ROYAL BOROUGH OF GREENWICH

Follow us on twitter @greenwichlibs

Please return by the last date shown

Thank you! To renew, please contact any
Royal Greenwich library or renew online at
www.better.org.uk/greenwichlibraries

passing verbal reasoning tests

Rob Williams

PEARSON

Harlow, England • London • New York • Boston • San Francisco • Toronto • Sydney
Auckland • Singapore • Hong Kong • Tokyo • Seoul • Taipei • New Delhi
Cape Town • São Paulo • Mexico City • Madrid • Amsterdam • Munich • Paris • Milan

PEARSON EDUCATION LIMITED

Edinburgh Gate
Harlow CM20 2JE
United Kingdom
Tel: +44 (0)1279 623623
Web: www.pearson.com/uk

First edition published 2014 (print and electronic)
© Pearson Education Limited 2014 (print and electronic)

The right of Rob Williams to be identified as author of this work has been
asserted by him in accordance with the Copyright, Designs and Patents Act 1988.

Pearson Education is not responsible for the content of third-party internet sites.

ISBN: 978–1-292–01545–3 (print)
　　　978–1-292–01547–7 (PDF)
　　　978–1-292–01548–4 (ePub)
　　　978–1-292–01546–0 (eText)

British Library Cataloguing-in-Publication Data
A catalogue record for the print edition is available from the British Library

Library of Congress Cataloging-in-Publication Data
Williams, Robert, 1967-
　Brilliant passing verbal reasoning tests / Rob Williams. -- First edition.
　　pages cm. -- (Brilliant)
　ISBN 978-1-292-01545-3 (pbk.)
1. Verbal ability--Testing. 2. Reasoning (Psychology)--Testing. 3. Reading
comprehension--Ability testing. 4. Employment tests. I. Title. II. Title: Passing
verbal reasoning tests.
　BF463.V45W55 2014
　153.9'3--dc23

2014021571

10 9 8 7 6 5 4 3 2 1
18 17 16 15 14

Print edition typeset in 10/14pt by 3
Cover design by David Carroll & Co.
Print edition printed and bound in Malaysia (CTP-PPSB)

NOTE THAT ANY PAGE CROSS REFERENCES REFER TO THE PRINT
EDITION

Contents

About the author

Rob Williams is a chartered occupational psychologist with over 20 years' experience in the design and delivery of ability tests. Having worked for several of the UK's leading test publishers, he has written many verbal reasoning tests and presented his research at home and abroad. Today he heads up Rob Williams Assessment Ltd, an independent company specialising in assessment for recruitment. Rob has run hundreds of assessment centres for numerous public sector organisations and private companies – giving him valuable insight into how testing is used in a wide range of businesses. When he's not working, Rob enjoys spending time with his two young daughters, going to the cinema and playing tennis.

To find out more, see **www.robwilliamsassessment.co.uk**

Acknowledgements

I would like to thank Anne Marie for her help with this book. Also my daughters Eve and Rose for the stories that they love to tell and write.

Foreword

S trange things, multiple choice tests. I remember sitting school exams and having a sense of relief at one being 'only' a multiple choice test as if it was somehow a lot easier than having to construct something from scratch or have to actually think about an answer.

Well, that may be true. But there is a resultant false sense of security here that usually means one does less preparation for it because we know we can just guess if we don't know the answer. I don't recommend this as a strategy, however. At least, it never did me any good. Guessing is strictly overrated and if you are in competition with others (and who isn't these days?), then you will always be up against people who don't have to.

Luckily, when it comes to that all-important verbal reasoning test, there is another option. Read this book. Oh, and practise. There is a good reason for this. While our true verbal reasoning ability essentially remains fairly stable (unless we are actively working on it) we can make a large difference in our test results in being more test-aware – having a set of strategies in place to make sure we perform as well as we are able. This does not mean that the test itself is unreliable – far from it, in fact. It just means that having those strategies results in your score being more likely to reflect your true ability. All the 'process' mistakes have been ironed out and what is left is the 'content' – your real verbal reasoning ability. It is an unfortunate truth that no matter how good the test itself is, your score is not going to reflect how good you actually are unless you know how to perform at your best from a standing start, as it were. And this is where this book comes in.

Understanding how to both analyse and interpret written information is key to the vast majority of graduate (and increasingly, non-graduate) jobs out there. We build these skills slowly through our education, our interactions with those around us and also our reading, but, like most things, if we don't make a conscious effort to grow our skills, they tend to remain stubbornly and unreasonably static – or worse, actually reduce. This is why this book is needed. We don't fulfil our true potential in assessments because of factors that have little to do with our true ability – lack of familiarity with testing under time pressure and nervousness being just two.

In my 15 years as an occupational psychologist I have tested many hundreds of individuals and talked to many of them about their strategies for completing the test at a feedback session. The answer was usually quite simple: there wasn't one. Well, not if you don't include 'guessing and hoping to be a statistical anomaly'. Having a clear strategy in your head before you sit down is your best chance of performing well on the day. And practice, practice, practice, of course.

You never know – that may just stack the odds in your favour. And if that hasn't persuaded you, perhaps this will: tests of reasoning ability are among the most valid forms of occupational assessment there are. In other words, good scores on the test predict good job performance in the future better than most types of assessment. Which, of course, is why they are used.

And which is why you need this book.

Peter Storr, C. Psychol.
London

PART 1

Getting to grips with your test

CHAPTER 1

Getting started

You've probably bought this book because you are facing a verbal reasoning test. Perhaps you are worried that your verbal reasoning skills are not up to scratch. Maybe you are feeling nervous because it has been a long time since you've sat a formal test. Or it might be that you just want to get ahead of the competition by being better prepared. All of these are great reasons – they mean you are motivated to practise.

As a psychometrician I have written many different types of verbal reasoning test. This has given me insights into the strange world of test design, so throughout the first part of this book you'll find brilliant test-taking tactics and tips that really work. The second part of this book is packed with practice tests you can take to improve your verbal reasoning skills. In short, here are all the tools you need to maximise your verbal reasoning performance.

What's a verbal reasoning test?

A verbal reasoning test is a type of ability test, sometimes referred to as a psychometric or aptitude test. It is designed to measure specific verbal

> A verbal reasoning test is a type of ability test

abilities relevant for success in a particular course, profession or job. Verbal reasoning tests are an objective and accurate means of assessing a candidate's potential effectiveness whenever there is a verbal component to a particular job role or course.

When do I use verbal reasoning?

Reading comprehension is something that we all do every day in both our personal lives and at work. From newspapers and magazines to correspondence and company reports, you use your verbal reasoning skills to make sense of all types of writing. Whether you are aware of it or not, you use your verbal reasoning skills when following a new recipe, reading a notice at a train station, applying for a bank account, or browsing through holiday brochures.

Who needs good verbal reasoning skills?

As you've seen above, *everyone* needs to have basic verbal reasoning skills to survive daily life. And *good* verbal reasoning skills are a key prerequisite for many different jobs. Any job that involves frequent communication requires verbal reasoning skills. This includes not just written communication such as emails or reports, but also spoken communication. Let's have a look at a typical office environment and how different workers use verbal reasoning skills to perform their duties.

> *good* verbal reasoning skills are a key prerequisite for many different jobs

Administrative roles

A personal assistant's responsibilities typically include written correspondence, such as letters and emails, which need to use appropriate language for the intended audience. Administrative assistants may also need to check written documents and file these accurately. Good oral communication skills are also necessary, as administrative assistants often make arrangements over the telephone.

Customer service/sales roles

Effective oral communication is the key to handling customer queries or sales calls. Talking to customers on the phone or face-to-face demands a flexible communication style. For example, telesales personnel would be expected to respond differently to a customer making a complaint from one who represented a possible sale. Persuasive presentation skills also rely upon a solid foundation of verbal reasoning skills.

Graduate trainees

Recent graduates on a training scheme will apply their verbal reasoning skills whenever they interact or correspond with other members of staff. They need to match their verbal communication to different levels of seniority and adjust their communication style to suit the formality of the meeting or event. Graduates may also need to prepare business reports in language appropriate for their target audience.

Managers/directors

Most managers will need to use higher levels of verbal reasoning when reading or preparing reports. They need to be able to adapt their spoken and written communication style to the situation, whether addressing their subordinates or customers/clients. Other company reporting procedures, such as staff appraisals, also require clearly written documentation.

Senior managers and directors will need to use high-level verbal reasoning skills when analysing complex company reports, dealing with compliance issues and statutory obligations. Here there is a need for concise and accurate communication and an ability to discern meaning quickly.

Why do I need to take a test?

Verbal reasoning ability links to job performance, which is why verbal reasoning tests are now used as part of the selection criteria for certain professions and postgraduate degree courses in which it is essential to work effectively with verbal

Verbal reasoning ability links to job performance

information. Many medium-sized and large employers also make extensive use of ability tests – such as verbal reasoning tests – as part of their standard recruitment and promotion processes. The overall aim is for the best people to be selected – and the use of ability tests differentiates the high performers from the low performers. A well-designed verbal reasoning test is a reliable and consistent means of assessing the skills required for effective performance in that working environment.

Ability tests allow employers and university admissions offices to assess a large number of applicants for competitive positions in a standardised way. The same ability test can be given to all applicants and the results can be used as an efficient means of comparison. This standardisation makes the process much fairer than relying upon old-fashioned, unstructured interviews where every applicant would be asked different questions. Even if you don't like the idea of being tested on your verbal reasoning skills, at least you know that it is fair since everyone has to do the same test!

How are verbal reasoning skills assessed?

There are many, many different types of verbal reasoning test at a variety of difficulty levels. These range from a basic test of your understanding of words to critical reasoning tests which assess your comprehension of the different parts of an argued case. Verbal reasoning tests are continually updated and revised. Some question formats, such as those asking you to identify synonyms and antonyms, or to identify the odd word out of a group, are basic tests of your understanding of the English language. The most frequently used verbal reasoning test format, however, is a passage of text followed by questions, and that is the format used in many of the practice tests featured in Part 2 of this book.

How can I prepare?

There's a lot you can do to prepare. I'll say it many times throughout the course of this book: the best way to improve your performance is through practice. Furthermore, you'll get the most benefit if you practise with questions that mirror the exact test you are preparing to take.

> the best way to improve your performance is through practice

Most of the test questions will be multiple choice. Don't be fooled into thinking that this makes them easier. The answer options are deliberately designed to catch out those who guess or make sloppy errors.

How important is my test?

Broadly speaking, the earlier in an assessment process that you are being asked to complete a verbal reasoning test, the more important it is to pass. Candidates who do not pass are sifted out of the process, allowing employers to focus on applicants whose skills are most suitable for the job.

You may be taking a verbal reasoning test as part of an assessment centre procedure where many different types of exercise – such as interviews, group exercises, presentations, role plays and other psychometric tests – are combined. Here, the test is a part of several assessments and you will not be sifted out on the basis of the verbal reasoning test alone. That said, it is still important to pass – you don't want a poor performance in the test to let you down.

brilliant recap

- Everyone uses verbal reasoning skills in both written and spoken communication.

- Verbal reasoning tests are a fair and objective way to assess large numbers of candidates. They are used because they predict future performance at work.

- There are many different types of verbal reasoning test on the market, at varying levels of difficulty.

- The best way to prepare for a verbal reasoning test is to practise with questions that mirror your actual test format.

CHAPTER 2

Practice
makes perfect

ry approaching your upcoming verbal reasoning test like a running race. You wouldn't just turn up at the starting line and hope for the best, would you? Instead, you'd go out for training runs in the preceding weeks – starting with easy jogs then building up to faster sprints. On the race day you'd want to be rested, relaxed, and in peak physical and mental condition. Whether you are a beginner or an experienced test-taker you can benefit from more practice. So let's get down to work!

Why should I practise?

Practising questions is known to significantly improve your chances of passing a verbal reasoning test. Try to squeeze in as much advance practice as possible so you can improve your confidence and keep a clear head on the day. Continually review what you have learnt from practice test sessions so that you use your time most effectively.

When should I practise?

First think about how much time you can spare for practising. Then set aside the time so you can conduct as many practice sessions as possible over a period of several weeks or months. Set aside a particular time of day or week when your mind is most alert.

think about how much time you can spare for practising

I'd strongly advise against doing all your preparation in one huge hit. You will learn and retain much more if you undertake several practice sessions instead of one big one. At first it may seem as if you are only making small gains, but these small gains will soon add up to improved verbal reasoning skills.

How much practice do I need?

That depends on why you are taking the test and your current skill level. Your verbal reasoning test may be the key to a new job or a new stage in your life. Even if the outcome is not solely dependent on your verbal reasoning test score, it is worth maximising your practice opportunities when your future is at stake.

The time required to improve your verbal reasoning testing performance will vary between a few hours for those who are just a little bit rusty to several days for less experienced readers.

Where should I start?

If you don't already know exactly what type of verbal reasoning test you will be taking, you should find out as your first step. Knowing what to expect on your test day will give you a big advantage, so learn as much as you can about the test you are going to take. Your recruiting organisation may send you practice material in advance of your test. This may be in the form of sample questions, either online or in printed format. The information should also outline why the test is being used in the process and – most importantly – the exact nature of the test that you will be taking on the day.

This practice opportunity levels the playing field and gives everyone a fair chance – particularly important for people who have not taken a verbal reasoning test before. If practice material is not sent to you in advance, call your prospective employer and ask for information regarding the test you are going to complete.

Before taking a practice test

- Identify a quiet place to work where you are unlikely to be disturbed. It is important to find an environment where you can read quietly and really concentrate.
- Clear away anything that may distract you before starting.
- Turn your mobile phone off.
- Have a clock or watch handy to time how quickly you work.

During the practice test

Research has shown that most people's concentration levels drop off after 40–50 minutes so you should limit your practice session accordingly. Try to treat your practice session as a real test to help you get into the right mindset. This will help reduce any nerves on the test day.

> treat your practice session as a real test

- Make sure you read the instructions very carefully. If you misinterpret the instructions you could answer several – if not all – questions incorrectly.
- Work systematically through all the questions in the relevant section. Attempt every question: do not cherry pick or randomly select questions. The reason for this is simple – you need to identify whether there are specific types of questions where your performance would benefit from further practice.
- Read each word of every question, as misreading a question can cost you dearly.
- If you finish earlier than you expected, use this extra time as an ideal opportunity to go back and double-check any questions you were unsure about. The same rule also applies when you take your actual test.
- Challenge yourself to do more and more questions in each timed practice session to improve your speed.

Timekeeping techniques

It is essential to manage your time efficiently in the run-up to the test to ensure you fit in enough practice sessions. But how you use your time *during* the test is also extremely important, as during the real test you will be working under strictly timed conditions. You don't necessarily need to finish the test in order to pass, but you do need a certain number of correct answers, so it is essential to pace yourself.

Right at the start of the practice test, work out roughly how long you should be spending on each question. Try to ensure that you do not spend longer than this as you go through each question. Every 10 minutes or so, check the time remaining against the number of questions that you have left to answer.

> work out roughly how long you should be spending on each question

Aim to spend a sufficient amount of time on each question. That's the amount of time that you need to spend in order to get the answer correct. No more and no less.

After taking a practice test

- Circle any incorrect answers.
- Go through each answer explanation for those questions you got wrong.

Learn from your mistakes

Take heed of any errors that you make throughout your practice session. Make a mental note of where you went wrong so you can avoid making similar mistakes in future. It's all too easy to mess up when you are under pressure to perform.

Stretch yourself

Don't just focus on those practice questions that you can do quite easily – stretch yourself with harder questions. Undertake timed practice tests on a regular basis to get your brain used to working under pressure.

You might be tempted to review the answers without doing the practice questions yourself. This might seem like a quick win, but it isn't. It will save you the time needed to work your way through the questions but it *won't* improve your verbal reasoning skills.

Common concerns

How do I know if I am improving?

Effective feedback is the key to improving your overall performance. That means going through the answer explanations in detail. After each practice session, keep a record of how many questions you get right. Compare your performances so you can gauge your improvement over time.

Am I working at a steady pace?

Most tests are timed and you need to cultivate a focused and alert approach. Your first priority is to work accurately as there's no benefit in getting questions wrong. But remember that the person sitting next to you could pass because they answered more questions than you did in the time limit – even though they also got more questions wrong.

Am I avoiding careless mistakes?

If you find yourself making too many careless mistakes you clearly need to slow down. Yes, you need to work at a brisk pace, but the key is to find the fastest pace that allows you to get the answers right. It is also essential to read every word of every question very, very carefully to avoid sloppy mistakes.

Are any patterns emerging?

Look for trends. Do you tend to make more mistakes at the beginning of your practice session? This could be a consequence of nerves. You need to work on achieving a high state of mental alertness immediately and giving the test 100 per cent focus as soon as you start work.

Are you making more mistakes near the end of your practice session? This could be because you are rushing the last few questions. You need to work steadily and maintain concentration throughout an entire test.

I'm not getting any better

Are you clear on why you are getting questions wrong? This is key to improving – you need to learn from your mistakes. It's vital to know where you need to improve most. If you are unaccustomed to a particular type of question it makes sense to spend additional time getting comfortable with these questions. Don't assume that you can pass without learning how to do that sort of question.

you need to learn from your mistakes

The questions are too difficult for me

In order to improve your score you need questions that mirror the difficulty level of the real test you'll be taking. The practice tests in Part 2 increase in difficulty, so start with the easiest questions and work your way up to the more difficult questions in the subsequent chapters.

 **recap**

Do

✔ Practise right up to the day before you are going to be taking your test.

✔ Familiarise yourself with the test you will be taking so you can tailor your practice sessions accordingly.

✔ Eliminate distractions so you can concentrate as you practise.

✔ Work at a brisk pace and always keep an eye on the time.

✔ Focus on understanding why you keep getting particular questions wrong and on avoiding any sloppy mistakes.

Don't

✘ Rely on one big practice session. Multiple practice sessions, limited to 40–50 minutes, will be more effective long term.

✘ Make sloppy mistakes. Read the instructions carefully, as well as each word of every question.

✘ Review the answer explanations without attempting to do the practice tests yourself.

✘ Assume that you can pass the test by avoiding the types of question that you find most difficult.

✘ Forget to double-check your answers if time permits.

CHAPTER 3

Mastering reading comprehension

Most verbal reasoning tests have a reading comprehension format. This involves reading a passage of text and then answering questions associated with the passage. You probably remember doing a similar exercise at school. However, the most difficult reading comprehension questions won't ask you to simply repeat back information exactly the way you read it in the passage. Understanding what is being asked is just one of the ways that your verbal reasoning is being assessed.

Learn the right steps

There is a knack to approaching these passage-based questions. It's a bit like learning a dance routine. Just as learning to tango involves following a sequence of steps, applying certain steps to each question can improve your verbal reasoning test scores. So, let's dance!

Step 1
Skim read the passage to get a rough idea of its content.

Step 2
Skim read the questions to get a rough idea of the level of difficulty and the sorts of things that you are going to be asked.

Steps 1 and 2 will prepare you for the level of complexity and the time that you need to spend answering the questions.

Step 3

Read the passage again!
Go through the passage again but read it more carefully this time. Do not spend time trying to memorise the details. Instead, think in broad terms about the different areas that the passage is covering. Try to make mental notes about where the specific pieces of information relating to each area are located in the passage.

Step 4

Try to get a broad sense of what you are going to be asked in each question and to know where this information was covered within the passage. Ask yourself: *Am I in a suitable position to answer the questions?* For more complex passages the answer to this will be no. Read the passage a third time. Try to identify the pieces of information in the passage that seem particularly important. Ask yourself the following broad questions as you read through:

- What point(s) is/are being made in the introductory statement?
- What does the main body of the text explore/detail?
- What details are provided in the final statement(s)?
- If there is a summary at the end of the passage, what point, if any, is it making?

Step 5

Ask yourself again: *Do I have a sufficient understanding to answer the set of questions?* If the answer is yes, then you are ready to carefully read the first question. You may only need to read the passage in full twice if you already know where to find the relevant information. Remember that the passage will always be there for reference so you don't need to memorise it.

But I'm no expert on this subject!

Don't worry if the subject matter in the passage is unfamiliar to you. Many of the passages you read will be about areas in which you have no interest or background knowledge. Nor do you need to apply any outside knowledge of the subject. Remember that your answer must be based solely on the information presented in the passage. Don't let your answer be clouded by any background knowledge that you

> your answer must be based solely on the information presented in the passage

may bring to bear on the question. A reading comprehension task requires you to extract the relevant information from the passage. Each question will relate to a particular part, or parts, of the passage. You will need to ferret out smaller pieces of information contained somewhere within the text to answer the question correctly.

Understanding the answer options

Many passage-based comprehension tests have three answer options: True, False and Cannot tell. Sounds obvious enough, right? Actually, it is surprisingly easy to get confused – especially about 'Cannot tell'. So let's just review what each option means.

- True means the statement is true *or* that it follows logically from the information given in the passage.
- False means the statement is false – based *only* on the information given in the passage.
- Cannot tell means you cannot say whether it is true or false because there is insufficient information given in the passage.

Remember that your answer must be based on the information given in the passage alone. If the test format has different answer options for each question then you must read through *all* of them to find the one that most closely answers the question. Be wary of selecting the first answer that seems true – or right – to you.

The microscope technique

The text passage may look very long to you but don't be put off by this. You may not even have questions relating to every sentence in the passage. Concentrate on examining the key sentences in as much depth as possible.

> Concentrate on examining the key sentences

One helpful way to approach a passage is to imagine yourself using a microscope or camera lens. You start with a wide setting to look at the whole passage and then the questions. This gives you a broad picture, or a general understanding of what's in the passage. If you find this difficult to do, try writing out the main theme or themes of passages before answering the questions. There won't be time to do this in an actual test situation but it's a good technique for training you to think about the big picture. Now focus the microscope (or camera lens) onto a specific part of the passage. For each question you need to zoom in to the relevant section to get the detail that you need. If you know which part of the passage the question is asking about, you are already well on your way to answering the question. You know where to find the vital clues.

Key words

Watch out for certain key words and phrases in either the passage or question (or both!). These key words often act as the link between different pieces of information. In many cases they qualify the information that has been given. When you come across key words you need to focus on their precise meanings. You are being tested on reinterpreting the passage so ask yourself: is there *exactly* the same emphasis in both the passage and question?

1. Contrast words

Contrast words and phrases (e.g. *however, although, but, whereas, alternatively, despite, rather, unless, instead, while, nevertheless, on the other hand, on the contrary, yet, at the same time, conversely*) are used to highlight differences. Contrast words make a transition between two clauses, or parts of a sentence, and emphasise a contrast in ideas or information.

Example:
Spain has always been a popular tourist destination, **however** *it now faces competition from cheaper resorts in other countries.*

You need to pay careful attention to the information that follows the contrast word as it is often the key to answering the question.

Is the answer to the following statement True, False or Cannot tell? *Spain is unrivalled as a tourist destination.* The answer is False. The sentence says that Spain has always been popular, but goes on to say that it now faces competition.

2. Propositions

There are certain words and phrases that you need to treat as propositions. Don't be misled into thinking that they are facts. These include the following: *claims, suggests, advocates, recommends, advises, offers, proposes, believes* and *considers*. Treat these words with caution as they indicate a subjective statement based on one person's opinions rather than absolute evidence.

Example:
The author **claims** *that his book will improve your verbal reasoning test performance.*

Is the answer to the following statement True, False or Cannot tell? *This book will improve your verbal reasoning test performance.*

Yes, there is a very good chance that this book will improve your performance if used properly, but this is not a fact so the answer has to be Cannot tell.

3. Comparisons

Be on the look-out for comparative adjectives. These are words that compare two or more things. At the simplest level, these are superlatives such as *most*, *highest*, *biggest* and *least*. But there are other words for making comparisons e.g. *more*, *lower* and *less*.

Example:
*There is **less** unemployment in the UK today than at any other point in the past decade.*

If asked whether the following statement is True or False – *Unemployment rates are currently lower than they were five years ago* – the answer would be True. If there is *less* unemployment today than at any point over the past ten years, then it follows that unemployment rates are lower than they were five years ago.

4. Absolutes and generalisations

Adverbs such as *never* or *always* compare how frequently something occurs. Be alert for any words that imply something absolute, such as *no*, *never*, *none*, *always*, *every*, *entire*, *unique*, *sole*, *all*, *maximum*, *minimum* and *only*. Don't confuse them with generalisations, such as *many*, *almost always*, *some*, *nearly*, *usually*, *seldom*, *regularly*, *generally*, *frequently*, *typically*, *ordinarily*, *as a rule*, *commonly* and *sometimes*. These generalisations create something of a grey area where a fact only applies some of the time. This is an important distinction. Just because something *usually* happens does not mean you can assume it *always* happens. It is important to recognise these words and interpret them accurately. Some words are relatively low generalisations, such as *a few, a little,* and *only some.* Similarly, *unlikely* and *infrequent* tell you that there is still a slight chance, which is not the same as *impossible.*

Example:
Research shows that excessive television viewing **usually** *damages a child's concentration.*

If faced with the statement: *Excessive television always damages a child's concentration* you might be tempted to answer True. The answer is in fact False – because the word *usually* tells you that this is a high possibility, not a guaranteed effect.

So, to summarise: don't assume that *usually* means the same as *always.* In the world of verbal reasoning tests such words are miles apart!

5. Cause and effect

After doing lots of practice tests you will come to recognise cause and effect words and phrases. These include: *since, because, for, so, consequently, as a result, thus, therefore, due to* and *hence.* It is a good idea to focus on these as often a question will ask you to interpret how these words have been used to link different aspects of an issue or argument together. There are subtle differences between these words and phrases, as some signal stronger causal relationships than others. A word like *because* indicates a direct causal link. The word *so* also joins facts together but does not necessarily mean that it was the first fact that led to the second.

Examples:
Consider the following two examples:

1 **As a result** of oversubscription, Adam did not get a place on the philosophy course.

2 The philosophy course was oversubscribed **so** Adam enrolled in a different class.

What is the answer if you are asked: *Did Adam get a place on the philosophy course?* In the first example, you know that he did not. The second example is more ambiguous. Perhaps Adam got a place, but opted out of the overcrowded course.

Be careful not to mix up causal words with sequential words such as *then*, *next*, *after* and *later*. These words indicate a chronological sequence rather than a causal effect. For example, *then* does not imply that one thing caused another to happen, only that it happened afterwards.

6. Speculation

Look out for words or phrases indicating speculation, such as *perhaps*, *probably*, *possibly* and *maybe*. Words such as *may*, *might* and *can* also point to the possibility of something happening. You need to tread carefully with such phrases – they do not mean the suggested outcome is guaranteed, only that it is a possibility.

Example:
If you are told: *The team will probably win the championship*, you should not interpret this as meaning that the team will *definitely* win. It is just speculation, even if there are good reasons for making that prediction.

7. Addition

A question may ask you to add something up, for example, the number of options or a number of instances. Stay on the alert for any addition words and phrases, such as *also*, *again*, *in addition*, *as well as*, *besides*, *coupled with*, *alternatively*, *moreover* and *furthermore*. Also, be sure to look for more options or instances appearing later in a passage.

Example:
*Conglomerate Plc announced redundancies in its accounts team, **as well as** job losses in its logistics and human resources departments.*

You may be asked to say whether the following statement is True or False: *Conglomerate Plc made redundancies in three parts of its business.* The answer would be True because the statement mentions job losses in accounts, logistics and human resources.

Other ways to improve your reading comprehension

Although the practice test questions in Part 2 are the best way to improve your verbal reasoning test performance, there are many other ways that you can turn everyday life into practice opportunities. Applying some – or all – of the suggestions below will not only boost your reading comprehension skills but also introduce you to a wider range of reading materials and help you cultivate a richer vocabulary. Getting comfortable with complex texts should enable you to approach your test with the highest possible level of confidence.

- Read a daily newspaper. If you already do this, switch to a newspaper at a higher reading difficulty level than your usual choice.

- When you come across articles about complex subjects spend time reviewing them. Ask yourself the following questions: What is the main point of each paragraph? Are both sides of an argument presented? What conclusion, if any, does the article come to?

- If you usually avoid the opinion and comment pages of broadsheets or magazines, then give them a go. These sections often contain challenging debates on popular subjects that require you to analyse the pros and cons of an issue.

- Visit your local library and select a range of books from different sections, especially the non-fiction shelves. Biographies, business books and technical titles will provide you with a broad range of reading material, just as verbal reasoning test questions will be drawn from a wide spectrum of topics.

 recap

● Approach passage-based questions in a systematic way so that you
  follow the line of reasoning.

● Be sure you understand the answer options.

● Answer the questions based only on information given in the passage.
  Do not let your own opinions or knowledge influence the way you
  answer.

● Look out for key words and phrases – they are often vital to interpreting
  the passage and answering the questions.

● Look for opportunities to improve your reading comprehension in your
  daily life.

CHAPTER 4

Sharpen
your critical
reasoning
skills

When you're shopping online, you use your critical thinking skills when you decide which product to buy based on reading multiple reviews. You also use these skills when you try to win an argument by backing up your point of view with facts and evidence. Critical reasoning skills allow you to consider different perspectives on an issue – whether it's given in conversation, on TV or radio, or in written communication. When you distinguish between facts and subjective opinions and perceive the logical consequences from a stated position, you are using your critical thinking skills. You will also need to use these skills when taking high-level verbal reasoning tests.

> Critical reasoning skills allow you to consider different perspectives on an issue

What is critical thinking?

Critical verbal reasoning is quite literally applying a critic's eye (i.e. critical analysis) to verbal information. It encompasses the logical analysis of the following features of complex written arguments and viewpoints: assumptions, inferences, opinions, facts and interpretations.

The term 'critical thinking' might sound a bit intimidating, but it is a skill you can learn. With the right practice, most individuals can develop their skills sufficiently to pass this type of verbal reasoning test.

Who uses these skills?

Everyone uses these skills sometimes, but some job roles specifically require a high level of verbal critical reasoning. Lawyers, in particular, need excellent critical thinking skills.

In fact, this is such an important prerequisite that a specific verbal critical thinking test – the LNAT – is used for entry to the legal profession.

Barristers, for example, use critical reasoning to:

- Remain objective and not to be prejudiced by their own opinions.
- Analyse large amounts of verbal information to build a case for their client.
- Identify the different ways legal doctrine can be interpreted.
- Present their evidence in court and state their conclusion based on it.

A judge will in turn use his critical thinking skills to balance all the evidence for and against the accused and reach a verdict.

The LNAT

- The National Admissions Test for Law (LNAT) was introduced internationally as a means of sifting the large number of applications for law degrees. LNAT performance provides unique and useful evidence of a candidate's reasoning ability and communication skills and helps to ensure that the application process is fair and objective.
- The test is divided into two sections. Part I is a verbal critical thinking test, while Part II involves essay writing.
- The LNAT allows applicants to demonstrate those critical thinking abilities - comprehension, interpretation, analysis, synthesis, deduction - which are a core skill for the legal profession. It is

- not designed to assess any knowledge of laws or any legal ability. Whilst there are seven subject areas for the passages (philosophy, education, law, politics, media, science and ethics), you are not expected to have any background knowledge of these.

- The onus is on written arguments, and assessing whether these arguments are strong or weak, contain assumptions, illogical conclusions and so on.

- You need to answer 42 questions and will be expected to interpret shades of meaning and the 'grey' areas within the arguments outlined in 12 passages.

- Although there is no pass mark, your LNAT grade is used as part of the selection process for taking a Masters in Law degree.

- Before taking the LNAT, it is highly advisable to practise and familiarise yourself with the test format in advance. There are plenty of excellent LNAT-specific practise testing books available, in addition to the practice test materials that are available on the official website. Coaches are available to hire, but self-directed and disciplined practice can prove equally fruitful.

- The official LNAT preparation website has a guide that is available for download at **www.lnat.ac.uk/lnat-preparation/ guide.aspx** and a practice test to try (**www.lnat.ac.uk/2008/ preparation/practice.html**). The Open University also has free, online writing courses (**www.open.ac.uk**).

The legal profession isn't the only field making use of critical reasoning tests. Senior managers in a variety of industries need excellent critical reasoning skills, and in the recruitment for such positions candidates may need to understand complex policy documents and to interpret legal requirements. Directors are responsible for both the detail of their annual company reports and for summarising their organisation's overall position. Marketing executives need to write PR briefs and press releases clearly and concisely.

Journalists also need to have a high level of critical reasoning skills. When commenting on a current affairs debate, a journalist will typically present all sides of the argument. After careful thought, and backed up by evidence, they then commit their own analysis to the page.

Watson-Glaser Critical Thinking Appraisal®

The Watson-Glaser Critical Thinking Appraisal measures critical thinking skills and the capacity for solving problems. The test takes approximately 35–40 minutes to complete, either online or in paper-and-pencil format. It is most commonly used for student selection and for either managerial selection or identifying senior managerial potential.

The critical reasoning questions in the Watson-Glaser Critical Thinking Appraisal are divided into five sections. Each section's type of critical verbal reasoning test is described below.

Assumptions A passage is followed by a set of statements that ask the candidate whether any of a series of assumptions has been made by the passage, or not.

Analysing Arguments A contentious argument is presented and then has to be analysed. It is followed by a list of points in favour of and against the contentious position. Candidates need to determine how strongly each point relates to the argument made.

Deductions Candidates must evaluate a set of deductions from a passage of prose, determining if each deduction does or does not follow on from the information in the passage.

Inferences Candidates are presented with a list of possible inferences from a passage and must rate each one as true, false, possibly true, possibly false or whether they cannot say from the information provided.

> **Interpreting Information** From the evidence provided in a passage of prose, candidates must decide if each of a series of conclusions follows on logically.

Deduction vs inference

It's not just the person writing a newspaper article who needs to use critical thinking skills – the person reading the article needs to apply them too. Discerning readers will assess whether the journalist is making an argument based on facts or is putting forth a subjective opinion influenced by the newspaper's bias towards a particular political party or against a certain group of people. An astute reader always asks: does the writer's overall conclusion follow on from the evidence and facts presented?

Critical reasoning involves applying both inductive and deductive reasoning to arguments.

● Logical **deduction** or deductive reasoning involves linking statements together to reach a logically sound conclusion. If the argument's premises are true, then it is logically impossible for the conclusion reached to be false.

● Inductive reasoning, or **inference**, is based on discerning what is *probable* or what is *likely to be true*.

How do critical thinking tests work?

Critical thinking tests are high-level analytical tests that assess how you think about and process verbal information. These tests are typically used in addition to or in place of a verbal reasoning test for graduate and managerial assessment.

As with verbal comprehension tests, a passage of text is presented, followed by a few questions. The passage is likely to be longer and more complex than in other verbal reasoning test

> there is no requirement to learn any facts or material in advance

formats. The type of language used should reflect the job or course that is being applied for. All the information that you need will be presented to you – there is no requirement to learn any facts or material in advance of the test.

What kind of questions will there be?

There are three broad types of critical thinking question, as seen in the practice tests (in Chapter 9).

Interpretation questions:

- Which sentence best summarises the passage?
- Which word could be substituted for another in the passage?
- Which of the following words is the most suitable replacement?
- What is meant by the following term?
- Which facts are included in the passage?

Summary questions:

- What is the main point the passage is making?
- Which of the following statements best summarises the second paragraph?
- Which statement best summarises what the author is saying in the last paragraph?
- Which of these statements does not form part of the passage's argument?

Assumption and deduction questions:

- What can be inferred about X from the passage?
- Which of the following can be deduced from the passage?

- Which of the following assumptions is made in the passage?
- Which statements lend support to the passage's argument?
- Which of these opinions is expressed by the author?

How can I pass my test?

Improving the speed at which you can digest complex prose will help your test performance. As with other reading comprehension tests, you should read the passage quickly the first time to get a feel for the main points. Then read the passage a second time more carefully, mentally noting the key content of each paragraph. Focus on the core of the argument and its supporting evidence, together with the author's stance on the issue.

While you need to absorb the test passages as efficiently as possible, that does not mean that you need to rush your answers. Quite the opposite, since there will be many different question formats. It is very important to double-check that you are 100 per cent clear on what the question is asking for.

To pass a critical reasoning test you need to understand the development of an argument – in particular, which points provide factual support. Reading commentary on political, social and economic debates will certainly improve your understanding.

> you need to understand the development of an argument

As you read such material, ask yourself:

- How are an individual's opinions and factual evidence expressed?
- Is there one or more argument? One or more conclusion?
- Are there any assumptions being used to make a conclusion?

● Is each piece of information reliable? Would you draw the same conclusion yourself?

● What additional information would you need to frame a counter-argument?

Take care when interpreting the meaning of complex words, particularly when you are being asked to make a judgement on the basis of a shade of meaning. Do not let your own general knowledge lead you astray. It's vital that you do not let any of your personal opinions or your general knowledge influence your answers even slightly. This recommendation applies even if it seems that the correct answer is in direct contradiction to what you know or believe to be true.

brilliant recap

● Critical reasoning tests are used to assess senior managerial candidates and for law school admission.

● Look for statements which are not supported by any facts.

● Separate facts from inferences and opinions and make logical deductions from a passage of text. Do not let your opinions influence your answer.

● Identifying the implications of a factual statement.

CHAPTER 5

Succeed on test day

You've now learned how to approach verbal reasoning tests and it is nearly time to put them into action. But before that, let's have a look at the test-taking process in general. Being fully aware of what to expect will help allay any jitters.

What will I be told in advance?

You should have been provided with the following information, in keeping with best practice:

- logistical information, such as directions about how to get to the test centre;
- advance notice that you will be taking a verbal reasoning test, including the length of time that the test will take to complete;
- an explanation of the testing process;
- the part that the test will play in the overall process, including who will have access to your results;
- any feedback arrangements.

What if I have any questions or concerns?

If you feel that anything has not been adequately explained to you, or if you are uncomfortable with any aspect of these issues, then don't hesitate to get in touch with the contact name that has been supplied. Remember that your prospective employer or place of study will want to ensure that you are treated fairly throughout the testing process.

If you have a disability, then be sure to inform your prospective employer or educational establishment in advance if you require any adaptations to the testing process. It is likely that you would have been asked this question on your application form. You may also have been asked to complete a separate equal opportunities or monitoring form. Let them know how you have approached testing in the past and what provisions need to be made to ensure that you have equal access to the verbal reasoning test. This includes the format of the test, the medium through which it is communicated, and how it is communicated. Adaptations can be made to the verbal reasoning testing process whenever it is appropriate to do so, including an additional time allowance and having the questions delivered in Braille or large print.

Mental and physical preparation

If you have completed plenty of practice questions, familiarised yourself with your test format, and learned how to apply the strategies in this book, you should be feeling confident. On the day of your test you need to be able to concentrate 100 per cent on the test. A positive, confident mindset is key. Avoid letting any emotional factors distract or disturb you during the test. Instead of worrying, channel your energy in a positive way – by working as briskly as possible through the test questions.

> A positive, confident mindset is key

Mental preparation isn't enough – you need to prepare yourself for the test physically, too. You should aim to get a good night's sleep before the test as you will concentrate more effectively if you are fully rested.

On test day

While feeling a bit nervous is probably inevitable, there are measures you can take to ensure that you are as relaxed as possible on the day:

● Arrive with plenty of time to spare. Just as you would not be late for an interview, you should not be late for a test.

● Have everything that you will need with you, including such items as reading glasses and hearing aids if you need them.

● Take deep breaths and actually hold your breath for a couple of seconds before exhaling.

Test-taking tactics

Remember that you are not expected to get a perfect score. Even if you get several answers wrong you can still pass the test, as long as a relatively small number of incorrect answers is outweighed by a much larger number of correct answers. Also important is the number of other candidates' correct answers.

Here are some top test-taking tactics to help you maximise your performance.

● Be methodical and do not jump ahead. Start by looking at the first question, answer it and then move on to the next. It is important to concentrate on one question at a time.

● Rely on your intuition if you can't decide between two answers. Which was the first answer that you came to? Often it is best to stick with that answer.

● If you run out of time or you cannot answer some questions properly, you have nothing to lose by putting down an educated guess. The only exception is if your test is being negatively marked (meaning that you would lose a mark for getting each question wrong).

● The questions are all worth the same amount of credit, so
you should answer all the questions that you find easy first.

What if I get stuck?

If you find that you are spending too long on a particular question, don't get bogged down. We all come across questions that
we find difficult. The quicker you decide to cut your losses the
better, since that will give you more
time to work on questions that you
may find easier to answer. Give your
best guess and move on. Ensure that
you have marked the question so that you can go back at the end
of the test if there is still time to review your answer.

> don't get bogged down

It is important to note that you should only guess on questions that you have no possibility of answering correctly. Most
verbal reasoning tests have three possible answers – True, False,
Cannot tell – so you only have a one in three chance of guessing
correctly. With odds like that, you won't pass if you guess too
many questions!

Online testing

Online testing has been the dominant medium for the last
few years. Now a job application process is likely to involve
completing an online application form and uploading your
CV to taking an online test. All this information immediately
becomes available to your potential employer. Efficiently stream-
lined applicant processing, such as
the use of psychometric tests as an
early sift, has driven a shift away from
any old-fashioned, labour intensive,
paper-based recruitment processes.

> Online testing has
> been the dominant
> medium for the last
> few years

Here are the major differences from the traditional paper-and-pencil test administration:

1   You will not have a test administrator available to answer any questions or to manage any problems. An online contact will be made available for you to use. However, it's vital that you take your online test on a computer that has a reliable broadband connection.

2   The functionality of some online tests is fixed so that you cannot go back to a previous question.

3   Most online tests require you to put an answer down for each question, otherwise the test will not allow you to progress to the next question.

Tips for taking online tests

- As most online tests (for recruitment purposes) are completed at home, you are advised to make your home environment as professional as possible. Take the test when you are best able to concentrate and focus – without any interruptions. Such advice might appear quite basic. Still, a short lapse in concentration could reduce your score by a couple of marks – potentially the difference between a pass and a fail.

- You are allowed as much time as you like to read the instructions onscreen. Take as much time as you need to make sure that you are absolutely clear on what you are being asked to do as there is no administrator to answer your questions.

- You'll be the only person in the room, but that doesn't mean that you control the time allowed on the test. Once you have started, you need to complete the test in the allocated time. You can take a break whenever you need to but it will cost you valuable time.

- A well-designed online test will have been thoroughly tested to work on most computers. You should be told any technical requirements in advance. But if you do have an access problem at any stage, use the contact information provided onscreen or by the person who sent you the invitation.

- If you do not have internet access at home, think about alternative venues for taking the test. For example, you could complete the test on a friend or relative's computer or at your local library.

- Don't leave taking the test to the last minute just in case you run into any computer problems.

Adaptive tests

Adaptive tests are designed to measure your verbal reasoning ability as efficiently as possible. You answer your first question and if it's correct, you will then get a more difficult question. However, if you get it wrong, you will be presented with an easier question. Using this process, an adaptive test establishes the most difficult question that you can answer correctly. Of course, there are some complicated statistics involved which determine what are the optimal questions to ask each candidate.

adaptive test questions deliberately adapt to how you are performing

As the name implies, online adaptive test questions deliberately adapt to how you are performing as you progress through the test. So, if you are doing well, you will find that the questions get progressively harder. That can feel like a challenge since you are pushed until you reach the most challenging level you can. This is the level at which you – just like other candidates with your level of verbal reasoning – start to get questions wrong.

Are there any benefits?

● Adaptive testing has led to a reduction from typically 25–30 minutes to 15–20 minutes for some online verbal reasoning tests. So you can complete the test in less time.

● The online test will have a timer visible throughout which makes it easy for you to track your progress.

● Traditional tests would present you, for example, with a passage and then a mixture of easy, medium and difficult test questions relating to each passage. When you sit an adaptive test, after the first few questions you will find that the questions are matched roughly to your verbal reasoning ability level.

How will my test results be used?

Your verbal reasoning test may be one stage in a long recruitment process. It will be used to screen out unsuitable applicants who do not have the necessary level of verbal reasoning ability. This process is called a sifting out, or de-selection, process. In my experience where recruitment processes, such as assessment centres, use a verbal reasoning test, doing exceptionally well and being graded in the top 'A-band' will certainly make you stand out from other applicants.

A frequently asked question is: *What's the average score on a verbal reasoning test?* This will vary considerably across both different types of psychometric test and within the spectrum of easy to difficult verbal reasoning tests. That's why the test is being used in the first place – to differentiate between applicants in terms of their verbal reasoning ability. There are two main reasons why knowing an average test score can be misleading. These correspond to the two ways in which your test result will be used by a prospective employer:

> knowing an average test score can be misleading

1   Each individual's overall score is compared to those of
    a large group of hundreds – sometimes thousands – of
    similar applicants who have taken the same test before.
    This is the norm group – the normal range of scores that
    are typical of the type of people who sit the test. This way,
    your individual score is given in a meaningful way for that
    particular test.

2   At the same time, there is a particular group of applicants
    who took the test around the same time as you did.
    The pass mark is likely to be based on how these other
    applicants performed. It may go up or down depending
    upon the number of vacancies for a particular job or course
    or the number of people who have applied. Where there is a
    high number of annual applicants, for example on a popular
    graduate training scheme, then there is likely to be a cut-
    off score for the verbal reasoning test. However, this will
    vary somewhat from year to year – it is adjusted to ensure
    that the cut-off does not create any adverse impact due to
    gender or ethnic group differences amongst applicants.

Will I get any feedback?

Feedback should always be provided and may take several forms.
It is important to remember that it is your relative performance
that has been measured – meaning how your performance compared to those of the large norm group that have taken the test
before. You won't receive marks out
of ten or a percentage score, as you
might expect. Instead, your feedback
could be one of the following:

Feedback should
always be provided

- A standardised score such as a percentile. This is similar to
  a percentage but a percentile of 60 per cent means that you
  did better than 60 per cent of the norm group.

A band that compares you to the norm group – e.g. average or above average. Remember, the term 'average' refers to average within a group of people similar to you who have taken the test for similar reasons to yourself. Your results are not being compared to those of the general population. So, a 'slightly below average' or 'below average' grade does not mean that you are worse than everyone else in the general population.

Good luck!

By now, you hopefully know what to expect from your verbal reasoning test and have had plenty of opportunity to practise. As you've seen, there are a lot of different strategies that you can apply to test taking in general and verbal reasoning questions specifically. If you want a quick and easy way to remember some key points that have been covered, just think of the Three Big Cs:

- Concentration
- Confidence
- Continual practice

brilliant recap

- If you have special needs, get in touch with the contact provided well in advance of your test day.
- Don't make any assumptions - if anything is unclear check before proceeding.
- Remember that all questions are worth the same. The important thing is to answer as many correctly as you can.
- Only guess on questions that you have no possibility of answering correctly.
- Feedback should always be provided and can take different forms. It compares your performance to that of a norm group.

PART 2

Time to practise

CHAPTER 6

Warm up tests

Introduction

The first four practice tests in this chapter are designed to measure a candidate's basic literacy and understanding of the English language. Tests at this level assess the ability to construct sentences and understand the meaning of individual words. These basic literacy tests are typical of those that school leavers applying for jobs might be required to take, or those trying to gain entrance into the Armed Forces. They are used to determine whether someone applying for a service industry position, for example, can communicate effectively in English, or whether a would-be soldier can comprehend documents and follow written orders.

The last two practice tests in this chapter are pitched at a higher difficulty level. Like the practice tests in the subsequent chapters, which are aimed at the graduate level and above, the fifth warm up practice test uses the passage of text format. The sixth practice test in this chapter assesses the ability to use grammar correctly and mirrors the grammar section of the Qualified Teacher Status (QTS) Literacy Test. Passing this test is a prerequisite for attaining Qualified Teacher Status, as effective communication – both written and spoken – is essential to the teaching profession.

If you know you will be taking a graduate-level verbal reasoning test, you may wish to skip ahead to the next chapter. However, if it has been a while since you sat a test, you may find completing the tests in this chapter a useful warm up exercise.

Instructions for warm up practice test 1

Read the sentence and then answer a question associated with it.

Example:

Johnny is less confident than Sue.

Who is more confident?

The first thing you need to focus on is the word or words that connect the two people. In the example above, the linking words are **less confident**. The next thing you need to do is decide the direction of the comparison being made. Once you have established this, answering the question is easy. If Johnny is **less** confident than Sue, it follows that Sue is **more** confident. So the answer is Sue.

Instructions for warm up practice test 2

Review the set of three words presented in each question. You need to determine which two words are connected. These two words could be connected because they mean the same thing (or almost the same thing) or because they mean the opposite thing. The answer is the third word – the odd one out. The first thing that you need to do is find the connection between two of the words. You might think that there are endless possibilities but most of the time the connection will be quite simple.

Example 1

Tame   Wild   Shoes

Shoes is the odd one out because tame and wild are **opposites**.

Example 2

Apple Dog Banana

Dog is the odd one out because apple and banana belong to the **same category** – they are both fruit.

Example 3

Rough Bumpy Clever

Clever is the odd one out because rough and bumpy mean the same thing – they are **synonyms**.

Instructions for warm up practice test 3

For each sentence that you are given, choose the correct word from the five multiple choice answer options. The test looks at how words are connected, such as opposites and synonyms, as well as other relationships between words. For example: spade is to gardener as wrench is to plumber. The connection is that a spade is a tool used by a gardener, while a wrench is a tool used by a plumber.

Focus on working accurately while also trying to complete as many questions as you can. You need to be able to complete at least three questions per minute. Time yourself and see how close you are to achieving this benchmark.

Instructions for warm up practice test 4

This verbal ability test assesses your ability to understand the meaning of words and the relationships between words. There are four different types of questions:

1) The first type of question gives you a short word and five other short words in brackets. The word outside the bracket

will go with only four of the words inside the bracket to make longer words. The answer is the word it will **not** go with.

Example:

Dis (play   rupt   may   able   rule)

The answer is **rule**, because display, disrupt, dismay, and disable are all words, but disrule is **not** a word.

2)   The second type of question gives you five words. The answer is the one word that describes or includes **all** the other words in its category.

Example:
A tennis
B rugby
C sport
D football
E hockey

The answer is **sport**, because all the other words are all different types of sport.

3)   The third type of question gives you a sentence with a missing word. You must decide which word from the answer options best completes the sentence.

Example
Considering how much we paid for the holiday, we were disappointed to be staying in such a ..... hotel.

A fancy
B shabby
C luxurious
D scenic
E historic

Shabby best completes the sentence, because the other words would not give reason for disappointment.

4) The fourth type of question gives you five sentences, four of which have the same meaning. The answer is the question that has a **different** meaning.

Example:
A Sam made a bet with Jess and won.
B The winner of the bet was Sam.
C Jess won the bet she made with Sam.
D Jess was not the bet's winner.
E Sam was the winner of the bet.

The answer is **C. Jess won the bet she made with Sam.** All the other sentences say, in slightly different ways, that Sam was the winner.

Instructions for warm up practice test 5

Read the short passage of text, which is followed by a number of related questions. Decide which of the multiple choice answer options is correct – based **only** on the information presented to you in the passage. You should aim to spend less than a minute on each question. Time yourself and see how close you are to achieving this benchmark.

Instructions for warm up practice test 6

Read the four sentences, then identify the only one that is grammatically correct. Look out for common errors, such as wrong verb tenses, incorrect use of determiners and comparisons, and lack of agreement – for example, a singular subject with a plural verb.

Warm up practice test 1

1) Peter is a faster runner than Paul.
   Who is the slower runner?
   A Peter
   B Paul

2) Raj has a more expensive watch than Jean.
   Who has the more expensive watch?
   A Raj
   B Jean

3) Sally is better at football than Lisa.
   Who is the better footballer?
   A Sally
   B Lisa

4) David is a faster typist than Pauline.
   Who is the slower typist?
   A David
   B Pauline

5) Mohammed reads more books than Gene.
   Who reads less?
   A Mohammed
   B Gene

6) Siri is brighter than Penny.
   Who is brighter?
   A Siri
   B Penny

7) Stephen is a stronger swimmer than Sarah.
   Who is the weaker swimmer?
   A Stephen
   B Sarah

8) Philip is more talented than Roger.
   Who has less talent?
   A Phillip
   B Roger

9) Graham is not as quick at maths as Harold.
   Who is slower at maths?
   A Graham
   B Harold

10) Alfred is quicker than Harry.
    Who is slower?
    A Alfred
    B Harry

11) Lisa is better at sports than Asha.
    Who is less good at sports?
    A Lisa
    B Asha

12) Vincent is not as good a cook as Gordon.
    Who is a better cook?
    A Vincent
    B Gordon

13) Jack is not as good a gardener as Nasim.
    Who is the lesser gardener?
    A Jack
    B Nasim

14) Ada is not as outgoing as Zack.
    Who is more outgoing?
    A Ada
    B Zack

15) Isaac is not as good a pool player as Peter.
Who is the lesser pool player?
A Isaac
B Peter

16) Valery is not as strong a card player as Shoaib.
Who is the better card player?
A Valery
B Shoaib

17) Evelyn is friendlier than Amritpal.
Who is friendlier?
A Evelyn
B Amritpal

18) Richard is more academic than Freddy.
Who is less academic?
A Richard
B Freddy

19) Riya is older than Andy.
Who is younger?
A Riya
B Andy

20) Sarah has a smaller car than Jason.
Who has the bigger car?
A Sarah
B Jason

21) Manuel has a lower drive than Yasar.
Who has less motivation?
A Manuel
B Yasar

22) Gary earns more money than Malcolm.
    Who has a higher salary?
    A Gary
    B Malcolm

23) Raymond is less happy than Tarnjit.
    Who is sadder?
    A Raymond
    B Tarnjit

24) Chukwuma is faster than Dirk.
    Who is slower?
    A Chukwuma
    B Dirk

25) Patricia is less eager than Geoffrey.
    Who is keener?
    A Patricia
    B Geoffrey

Review your answers to practice test 1

1) B Paul

2) A Raj

3) A Sally

4) B Pauline

5) B Gene

6) A Siri

7) B Sarah

8) B Roger

9) A Graham

10) B Harry

11) B Asha

12) B Gordon

13) A Jack

14) B Zack

15) A Isaac

16) B Shoaib

17) A Evelyn

18) B Freddy

19) B Andy

20) B Jason

21) A Manuel

22) A Gary

23) A Raymond

24) B Dirk

25) B Geoffrey

Instructions for warm up test 2

Review the set of three words presented in each question. You need to determine which two words are connected. These two words could be connected because they mean the same thing, or almost the same thing, or because they mean the opposite thing. The answer is the third word – the odd one out. The first thing that you need to do is find the connection between two of the words. You might think that there are endless possibilities but most of the time the connection will be quite simple. Possible connections include being opposites (see practice question 2), belonging to the same category (see practice questions 12 and 24), or being synonyms (see practice question 22).

brilliant tip

Quickly and accurately work through as many of the questions as you possibly can. Don't make the mistake of going too slowly.

Warm up practice test 2

1)   hat   man   woman
      A hat   B man   C woman

2)   cool   arm   hot
      A cool   B arm   C hot

3)   beer   wine   pull
      A beer   B wine   C pull

4)   queen   computer   king
      A queen   B computer   C king

5)   fist   last   first
      A fist   B last   C first

6)   diamond   good   bad
      A diamond   B good   C bad

7)   loud   heavy   quiet
      A loud   B heavy   C quiet

8)   five   whisper   eight
      A five   B whisper   C eight

9)   green   keeper   blue
      A green   B keeper   C blue

10)   boy   girl   baby
      A boy   B girl   C baby

11)   town   sweat   city
      A town   B sweat   C city

12)   goat   wing   cow
      A goat   B wing   C cow

13)   fair   name   unfair
      A fair   B name   C unfair

14)   lake   jumper   river
      A lake   B jumper   C river

15)   bungalow   beef   lamb
      A bungalow   B beef   C lamb

16)   sad   happy   jeep
      A sad   B happy   C jeep

17)   water   gift   present
      A water   B gift   C present

18)   right   enable   left
      A right   B enable   C left

19)   knife   attack   fork
      A knife   B attack   C fork

20)   bench   major   minor
      A bench   B major   C minor

21)   hard   event   soft
      A hard   B event   C soft

22)   same   identical   cash
      A same   B identical   C cash

23)   goal   target   gate
      A goal   B target   C gate

24)   steel   join   copper
      A steel   B join   C copper

25)   take   prepared   unprepared
      A take   B prepared   C unprepared

Review your answers to practice test 2

1) A hat

2) B arm

3) C pull

4) B computer

5) A fist

6) A diamond

7) B heavy

8) B whisper

9) B keeper

10) C baby

11) B sweat

12) B wing

13) B name

14) B jumper

15) A bungalow

16) C jeep

17) A water

18) B enable

19) B attack

20) A bench

21) B event

22) C cash

23) C gate

24) B join

25) A take

Instructions for warm up practice test 3

For each sentence that you are presented with, choose the correct word from the five multiple choice answer options.

Focus on working accurately whilst also trying to complete as many questions as you can. Aim to complete at least three questions per minute. Time yourself and see how close you are to achieving this benchmark.

brilliant tip

If you do not recognise a word, ask yourself whether it looks like any other words that you know? If you are unsure of an answer, try to eliminate as many of the answer options as possible.

Warm up practice test 3

1) LUNCH is to EAT as BEVERAGE is to
   A CONSUME
   B DRINK
   C DROWN
   D SWALLOW
   E GLASS

2) TEPID means the same as . . .
   A WARM
   B HOT
   C COLD
   D BATH
   E WATER

3) FISHMONGER is to FISH as ESTATE AGENT is to
   A SHOP
   B COD
   C HOUSES
   D ANGLE
   E RENT

4) COHERENT is the opposite of
   A CONFUSED
   B ARTICULATE
   C VARIOUS
   D CONNECTED
   E RATIONAL

5) FEASIBLE is the opposite of
   A ACHIEVABLE
   B RATIONAL
   C IMPOSSIBLE
   D RISIBLE
   E EASY

6) PLANE is to PILOT as CAR is to
    A VEHICLE
    B DRIVER
    C PLAIN
    D AIRMAN
    E FLY

7) SIMPLE means the same as. . .
    A SAME
    B COMPLEX
    C CONFLICTING
    D EASY
    E FEASIBLE

8) REGULAR is the opposite of
    A FREQUENTLY
    B IRREGULAR
    C ALWAYS
    D UNIFORM
    E RECURRING

9) ROAD is to DRIVE as FOOTPATH is to
    A PASSAGE
    B ROUTE
    C FOREST
    D NAVIGATE
    E WALK

10) NOVEL means the same as . . .
    A NEW
    B HOVEL
    C UNORIGINAL
    D UNEASY
    E SELDOM

11) EQUITABLE is the opposite of
   A ALIKE
   B DOUBLE
   C UNFAIR
   D UNIFORM
   E EQUITY

12) PEN is to WRITE as ERASER is to
   A DRAW
   B PENCIL
   C INK
   D ERASE
   E PAPER

13) OPERATE means the same as . . .
   A USE
   B SURGEON
   C DISCLOSE
   D HOSPITAL
   E DIVEST

14) PLENTIFUL is the opposite of
   A MORE
   B BUMPER
   C BOUNTIFUL
   D SCARCE
   E UNLIKELY

15) JUDGE is to COURT as SAILOR is to
   A TAILOR
   B SEAMAN
   C LAWYER
   D MAGISTRATE
   E SHIP

16) SIMILAR means the same as . . .

    A OPPOSITE

    B ADDITION

    C COMPARABLE

    D EXACT

    E DIVERGENT

17) RAPID is the opposite of

    A WATERFALL

    B FAST

    C VAPID

    D SPEEDILY

    E LEISURELY

18) THERMOMETER is to TEMPERATURE as WATCH
    is to

    A HOT

    B HOUR

    C TEMPERAMENT

    D TIME

    E LOOK

19) ENTIRE means the same as . . .

    A COMPLETE

    B GLOBAL

    C FRACTION

    D ENTITY

    E PORTION

20) MEAN is the opposite of

    A EXACT

    B AVERAGE

    C GENEROUS

    D TIGHT

    E NASTY

Review your answers to practice test 3

1) B DRINK

2) A WARM

3) C HOUSES

4) A CONFUSED

5) C IMPOSSIBLE

6) B DRIVER

7) D EASY

8) B IRREGULAR

9) E WALK

10) A NEW

11) C UNFAIR

12) D ERASE

13) A USE

14) D SCARCE

15) E SHIP

16) C COMPARABLE

17) E LEISURELY

18) D TIME

19) A COMPLETE

20) C GENEROUS

Instructions for warm up practice test 4

This verbal ability test assesses your ability to understand the meaning of words and the relationships between words. There are four different types of questions:

1 The first type of question gives you a short word and five other short words in brackets. The word outside the brackets will go with only four of the words inside the brackets to make longer words. The correct answer is the word it will not go with.

2 The second type of question gives you five words. The answer is the one word that describes or includes all the other words.

3 The third type of question gives you a sentence with a missing word. You must decide which word from the answer options best completes the sentence.

4 The fourth type of question gives you five sentences, four of which have the same meaning. The answer is the sentence that has a different meaning.

Warm up practice test 4

1) The word outside the brackets will go with only four of the words inside the brackets to make longer words. Which one word will it not go with?

	A	B	C	D	E
be	(long	sides	hind	fore	ween)

2) Which word has a meaning that extends to or includes the meaning of all the others?

A beret

B cap

C hat

D fedora

E bowler

3) The sentence below has a word missing. Which one word makes the best sense of the sentence?

The house has a great location, but it is so ... that the buyer will need to renovate it completely before moving in.

A dilapidated

B modern

C expensive

D noisy

E attractive

4) The word outside the brackets will go with only four of the words inside the brackets to make longer words. Which one word will it not go with?

	A	B	C	D	E
rest	(less	ion	ate	ore	rain)

5) Which word has a meaning that extends to or includes the meaning of all the others?

   A semi-detached
   B terraced
   C detached
   D house
   E maisonette

6) Four of the five sentences have the same meaning. Which one sentence has a different meaning?

   A I ate my dinner already.
   B I have not yet eaten my dinner.
   C My dinner has already been eaten.
   D I have already eaten my dinner.
   E The meal that I ate was dinner.

7) The word outside the brackets will go with only four of the words inside the bracket to make longer words. Which one word will it not go with?

	A	B	C	D	E
con	(tent	trite	verge	dam	sort)

8) Which word has a meaning that extends to or includes the meaning of all the others?

   A dog
   B goldfish
   C pet
   D cat
   E horse

9) The sentence below has a word missing. Which one word makes the best sense of the sentence?

Even though she had won the lottery, Ellen remembered her poor childhood and remained ... with her money.

A extravagant

B neat

C bold

D kind

E thrifty

10) The word outside the brackets will go with only four of the words inside the brackets to make longer words. Which one word will it not go with?

	A	B	C	D	E
super	(star	sonic	idea	vision	natural)

11) Which word has a meaning that extends to or includes the meaning of all the others?

A vehicle

B car

C van

D bus

E taxi

12) Four of the five sentences have the same meaning. Which one sentence has a different meaning?

A The boy walked his dog in the morning.

B Before school, the boy walked his pet dog.

C The boy's dog was taken for a walk first thing.

D The dog was walked this morning by the boy.

E The boy still needs to walk his dog.

13) The word outside the brackets will go with only four of the words inside the brackets to make longer words. Which one word will it not go with?

	A	B	C	D	E
at	(tic	one	test	tune	tong)

14) Which word has a meaning that extends to or includes the meaning of all the others?

A red

B colour

C orange

D yellow

E green

15) The sentence below has a word missing. Which one word makes the best sense of the sentence?

The famous chef, who had a fiery temperament, was as renowned for his blistering ... as for his exotic recipes.

A ingredients

B reviews

C outbursts

D saucepans

E ovens

16) The word outside the brackets will go with only four of the words inside the brackets to make longer words. Which one word will it not go with?

	A	B	C	D	E
an	(gel	them	tics	den	on)

17) Which word has a meaning that extends to or includes the meaning of all the others?

A florist

B chemist

C baker

D shop

E butcher

18) The word outside the brackets will go with only four of the words inside the brackets to make longer words. Which one word will it not go with?

	A	B	C	D	E
inter	(cede	man	pose	mingle	face)

19) Four of the five sentences have the same meaning. Which one sentence has a different meaning?

A The shop is only open on the weekend.

B At the weekend, the shop is not open.

C The shop is not open on Saturday or Sunday.

D Every weekend the shop is shut.

E The shop is closed at the weekend.

20) The word outside the brackets will go with only four of the words inside the brackets to make longer words. Which one word will it not go with?

	A	B	C	D	E
in	(apt	burn	form	bred	active)

21) Which word has a meaning that extends to or includes the meaning of all the others?

A table

B furniture

C chair

D sofa

E bureau

22) The sentence below has a word missing. Which one word makes the best sense of the sentence?

After getting such terrible reviews on their opening night, the play's cast lacked ... as they prepared for the next show.

A concern

B tickets

C pity

D confidence

E drama

23) The word outside the brackets will go with only four of the words inside the brackets to make longer words. Which one word will it not go with?

	A	B	C	D	E
pass	(word	port	age	ion	eon)

24) Which word has a meaning that extends to or includes the meaning of all the others?

A flower

B daisy

C rose

D tulip

E daffodil

25) Four of the five sentences have the same meaning. Which one sentence has a different meaning?

A The weather continued to be cold and rainy.

B It is cold and wet outside.

C For the past few days, it has been cold and wet.

D Outside, it is cold and rainy.

E Tomorrow the weather will improve.

26) The word outside the brackets will go with only four of the words inside the brackets to make longer words. Which one word will it not go with?

	A	B	C	D	E
land	(scape	sort	slide	lord	mark)

27) Which word has a meaning that extends to or includes the meaning of all the others?

A potato

B carrot

C vegetable

D pea

E bean

28) Which word has a meaning that extends to or includes the meaning of all the others?

A apple

B chicken

C soup

D turkey

E food

29) Four of the five sentences have the same meaning. Which one sentence has a different meaning?

A Erica forgot to give Richard a birthday present.

B Richard did not receive a birthday present from Erica.

C Unfortunately, Erica had forgotten Richard's birthday present.

D Richard thanked Erica for the birthday present she gave him.

E Erica forgot to bring Richard's birthday present.

30) The word outside the brackets will go with only four of the words inside the brackets to make longer words. Which one word will it not go with?

	A	B	C	D	E
head	(age	first	room	phone	ache)

31) Which word has a meaning that extends to or includes the meaning of all the others?

A one

B five

C hundred

D number

E twenty

32) The sentence below has a word missing. Which one word makes the best sense of the sentence?

The scientist was normally very shy, but if you asked about his work he would become quite ... as he explained his experiments enthusiastically.

A reserved

B boring

C sincere

D animated

E rude

33) The word outside the brackets will go with only four of the words inside the brackets to make longer words. Which one word will it not go with?

	A	B	C	D	E
car	(go	ion	pet	mine	rot)

34) Which word has a meaning that extends to or includes the meaning of all the others?

A lawyer

B accountant

C profession

D doctor

E architect

35) Four of the five sentences have the same meaning. Which one sentence has a different meaning?

A Brian sold his stamp collection.

B Brian collects stamps.

C Brian has a stamp collection.

D The stamp collection belongs to Brian.

E The stamps have been collected by Brian.

36) The word outside the brackets will go with only four of the words inside the brackets to make longer words. Which one word will it not go with?

	A	B	C	D	E
am	(end	using	bush	steal	oral)

37) Which word has a meaning that extends to or includes the meaning of all the others?

A slipper

B shoe

C trainer

D sandal

E flip-flop

38) The sentence below has a word missing. Which one word makes the best sense of the sentence?

We would have been better off hiring a four-wheel drive, as the road through the mountains was winding and even more … in the snow.

A polluted

B scenic

C cold

D narrow

E dangerous

39) The word outside the brackets will go with only four of the words inside the brackets to make longer words. Which one word will it not go with?

	A	B	C	D	E
in	(deed	cur	bed	crease	corporate)

40) Which word has a meaning that extends to or includes the meaning of all the others?

A weather

B hot

C wet

D cold

E changeable

41) Four of the five sentences have the same meaning. Which one sentence has a different meaning?

A Fred made a cake for the fair.

B Fred bought a cake at the fair.

C At the fair, there was a cake made by Fred.

D Fred's cake was at the fair.

E A cake made by Fred was at the fair.

42) The word outside the brackets will go with only four of the words inside the brackets to make longer words. Which one word will it not go with?

	A	B	C	D	E
con	(sign	tail	tent	sent	fuse)

43) Which word has a meaning that extends to or includes the meaning of all the others?

A steel

B copper

C iron

D lead

E metal

44) The sentence below has a word missing. Which one word makes the best sense of the sentence?

When the clock struck midnight, the party's gracious hostess ... suggested that her guests should start heading home.

A cleverly

B softly

C wisely

D hurriedly

E tactfully

45) The word outside the brackets will go with only four of the words inside the brackets to make longer words. Which one word will it not go with?

	A	B	C	D	E
super	(vision	nil	market	intend	sonic)

46) Which word has a meaning that extends to or includes the meaning of all the others?

A trumpet

B instrument

C drum

D guitar

E flute

47) Four of the five sentences have the same meaning. Which one sentence has a different meaning?

A The teacher presented the pupil with the award.

B The pupil's award was given by the teacher.

C The pupil received the award from the teacher.

D The teacher was presented with an award by the pupil.

E The pupil won an award, which was presented by the teacher.

48) The word outside the brackets will go with only four of the words inside the brackets to make longer words. Which one word will it not go with?

	A	B	C	D	E
head	(light	way	stone	wind	fill)

49) Which word has a meaning that extends to or includes the meaning of all the others?

A book

B novel

C guide

D poetry

E biography

50) The sentence below has a word missing. Which one word makes the best sense of the sentence?

Historians have ... the mysterious rock formations at Stonehenge for generations, but remain uncertain about the ancient stones' original purpose.

A admired

B studied

C photographed

D visited

E enjoyed

51) The word outside the brackets will go with only four of the words inside the brackets to make longer words. Which one word will it not go with?

	A	B	C	D	E
inter	(view	lock	cede	lace	side)

52) Which word has a meaning that extends to or includes the meaning of all the others?

A apple

B pear

C fruit

D banana

E orange

53) Four of the five sentences have the same meaning. Which one sentence has a different meaning?

A My library book is due back today.

B Today is the day on which my library book is due.

C My library book is now overdue.

D Today my library book is due back.

E I must bring my book back to the library today.

54) The word outside the brackets will go with only four of the words inside the brackets to make longer words. Which one word will it not go with?

	A	B	C	D	E
super	(human	power	star	sonic	tend)

55) Which word has a meaning that extends to or includes the meaning of all the others?

A   antelope

B   giraffe

C   lion

D   animal

E   zebra

56) The sentence below has a word missing. Which one word makes the best sense of the sentence?

Jane has bought a very ... new computer with a wide range of different programmes, even though she only really needs it for basic functions such as word processing and email.

A   popular

B   dependable

C   sophisticated

D   sleek

E   heavy

57) Four of the five sentences have the same meaning. Which one sentence has a different meaning?

A   We are going to the seaside for our holiday.

B   The seaside is where we are going on holiday.

C   Last year we went on holiday to the seaside.

D   Our holiday will be spent at the seaside.

E   We will be spending our holiday at the seaside.

58) Which word has a meaning that extends to or includes the meaning of all the others?

A   plane

B   chisel

C   saw

D   hammer

E   tool

Review your answers to practice test 4

1)   E   ween

2)   C   hat

3)   A   dilapidated

4)   B   ion

5)   D   house

6)   B   I have not yet eaten my dinner.

7)   D   dam

8)   C   pet

9)   E   thrifty

10)   C   idea

11)   A   vehicle

12)   E   The boy still needs to walk his dog.

13)   E   tong

14)   B   colour

15)   C   outbursts

16)   D   den

17)   D   shop

18)   B   man

19)   A   The shop is only open on the weekend.

20)   B   burn

21)   B   furniture

22)   D   confidence

23) E   eon

24) A   flower

25) E   Tomorrow the weather will improve.

26) B   sort

27) C   vegetable

28) E   food

29) D   Richard thanked Erica for the birthday present she gave him.

30) A   age

31) D   number

32) D   animated

33) B   ion

34) C   profession

35) A   Brian sold his stamp collection.

36) D   steal

37) B   shoe

38) E   dangerous

39) C   bed

40) A   weather

41) B   Fred bought a cake at the fair.

42) B   tail

43) E   metal

44) E   tactfully

45) B   nil

46) B instrument

47) D The teacher was presented with an award by the pupil.

48) E fill

49) A book

50) B studied

51) E side

52) C fruit

53) C My library book is now overdue.

54) E tend

55) D animal

56) C sophisticated

57) C Last year we went on holiday to the seaside.

58) E tool

Instructions for warm up practice test 5

Here are the test instructions: *You will be presented with an intro-ductory passage. This passage comprises of one to three sentences followed by a number of statements. Read the passage then decide which of the multiple choice options is correct – based only on the information presented to you in the passage.*

The actual RAF test has twenty questions and allows you fifteen minutes to answer these. You need to be able to complete four questions on average every three minutes. Time yourself and see how close you are to achieving this benchmark.

Warm up practice test 5

A group of teenagers is planning a Saturday night trip to the cinema. Their local multiplex has a range of different films showing across different film genres.

- Nicola likes science fiction or fantasy films best.
- Hifzu likes comedy films best. Hifzu will not go to watch an action film.
- Carol likes thrillers, comedy and action films.
- Simon likes thrillers best.
- Peter will not go to see a romance film.

1) What type of film would suit Simon and Carol most?
   A romance
   B fantasy
   C action
   D thriller
   E comedy

2) Whose first preference is to see a fantasy or science fiction film?
   A Peter
   B Nicola
   C Hifzu
   D Carol
   E Simon

3) The five teenagers want to go and see a film together. Which film genres are not an option?
   A romance and action
   B fantasy and romance
   C fantasy and action
   D fantasy
   E thriller and action

4)   Who would like to go and see a comedy film?
    A Peter, Nicola
    B Hifzu, Simon
    C Hifzu, Carol
    D Peter, Carol
    E Simon, Nicola

5)   Who would prefer to see a romance film?
    A Peter
    B Nicola
    C Hifzu
    D Carol
    E can't tell

Mr Phillips is the Managing Director of an IT company based in Salford. He has three Directors who report to him – Mrs Kaur, Mr Patel and Mrs Salamon, who is the Director of Operations. Mr Patel is the Client Director. Mrs Jenkins supports Mrs Salamon within the Operations team. Mr Hifzu is the Deputy Client Director and reports to Mr Patel. Mrs Jenkins is the only administrator who works for the company. Mr Phillips, Mr Patel, Mrs Salamon, Mrs Jenkins and Mr Hifzu are all graduates.

6)   Who is best suited to completing administrative jobs?
    A Mr Phillips
    B Mrs Kaur
    C Mr Patel
    D Mrs Jenkins
    E Mr Hifzu

7)   Who is the only non-graduate who works for the company?
    A Mr Phillips
    B Mrs Kaur
    C Mr Patel
    D Mrs Jenkins
    E Mr Hifzu

8) Who works with the Director of Operations?
   A Mr Phillips
   B Mrs Kaur
   C Mr Patel
   D Mrs Jenkins
   E Mr Hifzu

9) Who takes charge of client accounts when Mr Patel is away on holiday?
   A Mr Phillips
   B Mrs Kaur
   C Mr Patel
   D Mrs Jenkins
   E Mr Hifzu

10) Who is the most senior member of staff?
    A Mr Phillips
    B Mrs Kaur
    C Mr Patel
    D Mrs Jenkins
    E Mr Hifzu

A family is considering which of five popular tourist attractions to visit on Sunday afternoon:

- The Tithe Museum is expensive but is the adults' first choice.
- Penny Park is the cheapest option and is also within walking distance but has a poor reputation for litter and graffiti.
- Speedy's Fun Fair rides are overpriced according to the guidebook, but are always popular with children.
- Seacombe Beach is too far to drive to in a day, but is accessible by public transport. It is the only option that has free entrance.
- The Peak National Monument has the highest number of star ratings in the family's guidebook, but the children are refusing to go.

11) Which is the cheapest option?
   A Tithe Museum
   B Penny Park
   C Speedy's Fun Fair
   D Seacombe Beach
   E Peak National Monument

12) Which attraction is the easiest to walk to?
   A Tithe Museum
   B Penny Park
   C Speedy's Fun Fair
   D Seacombe Beach
   E Peak National Monument

13) What option do the parents prefer?
   A Tithe Museum
   B Penny Park
   C Speedy's Fun Fair
   D Seacombe Beach
   E Peak National Monument

14) What would be the children's last choice?
   A Tithe Museum
   B Penny Park
   C Speedy's Fun Fair
   D Seacombe Beach
   E Peak National Monument

15) Which option has the highest rating?
   A Tithe Museum
   B Penny Park
   C Speedy's Fun Fair
   D Seacombe Beach
   E Peak National Monument

A newsagent offers a range of five newspapers. Newspapers B, D and E contain full TV programme listings for the week.

Newspapers A and D come with free celebrity magazines that are popular with teenage readers. There is a culture review section in newspaper B each day of the week. Newspaper D is the most expensive option. Newspapers C and D come with a section on residential properties for sale. Newspaper C is the least expensive. Newspapers A and E feature job listings every day of the week; E's are local listings and A's are national job listings. Newspapers A and E also have weekend editions.

Which newspaper would each of the following prefer to choose from this newsagent?

16) A teenager looking nationally for a job who does not have much money to spend on a newspaper.

    A newspaper A

    B newspaper B

    C newspaper C

    D newspaper D

    E newspaper E

17) A local resident who wants to look for local job listings on a weekend.

    A newspaper A

    B newspaper B

    C newspaper C

    D newspaper D

    E newspaper E

18) A married couple who want to read a culture section and also have a full TV guide in the newspaper that they buy.

    A newspaper A

    B newspaper B

    C newspaper C

    D newspaper D

    E newspaper E

19) A newcomer to the area who wants to buy the cheapest newspaper with local houses listed for sale in it.

   A newspaper A
   B newspaper B
   C newspaper C
   D newspaper D
   E newspaper E

20) An unemployed builder who wants to use his newspaper to look for a job as well as having a celebrity magazine to read afterwards.

   A newspaper A
   B newspaper B
   C newspaper C
   D newspaper D
   E newspaper E

Review your answers to practice test 5

1)   D thriller

2)   B Nicola

3)   A romance and action

4)   C Hifzu, Carol

5)   E can't tell

6)   D Mrs Jenkins

7)   B Mrs Kaur

8)   D Mrs Jenkins

9)   E Mr Hifzu

10) A Mr Phillips

11) B Penny Park

12) B Penny Park

13) A Tithe Museum

14) E Peak National Monument

15) E Peak National Monument

16) A newspaper A

17) E newspaper E

18) B newspaper B

19) C newspaper C

20) A newspaper A

Instructions for warm up practice test 6

You need to select the correct phrase or sentence to insert into a short passage. You will be given a choice of several alternatives, only one of which is grammatically correct. In the following practice questions, identify which sentence is grammatically correct.

brilliant tip

Remember, remember!

1   Carefully read and interpret the sentences – many of the options will be similar, and you need to pay close attention to detail in order to spot the errors.

2   Good grammar requires consistency. So check that the tenses, the pronouns, the case, and the person are consistent throughout the set of statements.

Warm up practice test 6

1

A) If the OFSTED inspectors do not see an improvement when they return to the school, the head will have to resign.

B) If the OFSTED inspectors do not see an improvement when they return to the school, the head will have had to resign.

C) If the OFSTED inspectors do not see an improvement when they return to the school, the head would have had to have resigned.

D) If the OFSTED inspectors do not see an improvement when they return to the school, the head would have resigned.

2

A) Child development as a field of study covers all kinds of subject.

B) Child development as a field of study covers all kind of subject.

C) Child development as a field of study covers different kinds of subject.

D) Child development as a field of study covers all kinds of subjects.

3

A) Considering how much revision the student did, her exam results could of been better.

B) Considering how much revision the student did, her exam results should of been better.

C) Considering how much revision the student did, her exam results should have been better.

D) Considering how much revision the student did, her exam results must have been better.

4

A)   We was prepared for the Christmas concert when the fire alarm went off.

B)   We were preparing for the Christmas concert when the fire alarm went off.

C)   We was preparing for the Christmas concert when the fire alarm went off.

D)   We will be prepared for the Christmas concert when the fire alarm went off.

5

A)   When the next academic year starts, there will be many new pupils, each of whom is learnt the school rules.

B)   When the next academic year starts, there is many new pupils who are each learning the school rules.

C)   When the next academic year starts, there are many new pupils to learn the school rules.

D)   When the next academic year starts, there will be many new pupils who will each learn the school rules.

6

A)   There are many books that pupils can take out of the library but their not allowed to take them out for more than two weeks at a time.

B)   There are many books that pupils can take out of the library but they're not allowed to take them out for more than two weeks at a time.

C)   These are the many books that pupils can take out of the library but their not allowed to take them out for more than two weeks at a time.

D)   Here there is many books that pupils can take out of the library but they're not allowed to take them out for more than two weeks at a time.

7

A) Me and the teacher looked over the solution to the maths problem.

B) The teacher showed myself how to solve the maths problem.

C) Myself and the teacher looked over the solution to the maths problem.

D) The teacher showed me the solution to the maths problem.

8

A) Children must remember to wear their plimsolls when you have PE classes.

B) Children are forgetting to wear plimsolls when you have PE classes.

C) Children must remember to wear their plimsolls when they have PE classes.

D) Children must not forget to wear your plimsolls to PE classes.

9

A) He and I are presenting a paper at a national teachers' conference next week.

B) Me and him are presenting a paper at a national teachers' conference next week.

C) He and me are presenting a paper at a national teachers' conference next week.

D) Him and myself are presenting a paper at a national teachers' conference next week.

10

A) Peter was the eldest of the two brothers.

B) Peter was the elder of the two brothers.

C) Peter was more older than his brother.

D) Peter was more elder than his brother.

11

A)   Every sort of book is available on how to raise your child.

B)   All sorts of book is available on how to raise your child.

C)   Every sort of book are available on how to raise your child.

D)   Each sort of books are available on how to raise your child.

12

A)   Of all the swimmers on the team this year, Alex is the faster swimmer.

B)   Of all the swimmers on the team this year, Alex is the most fast.

C)   Of all the swimmers on the team this year, Alex is the fastest.

D)   Of all the swimmers on the team this year, Alex is faster.

13

A)   It was the new teacher's stricter regime whom the parents preferred.

B)   It was the new teacher's stricter regime who the parents preferred.

C)   It was the new teacher's stricter regime that the parents preferred.

D)   It was the new teacher's stricter regime with which the parents preferred.

14

A)   After raising enough money at the summer fair, the new computer software was purchased by the PTA.

B)   After raising enough money at the summer fair, the PTA purchased new computer software.

C)   After raising enough money at the summer fair, the money was used by the PTA to purchase new computer software.

D)   After raising enough money at the summer fair, the new computer software was bought by the PTA.

15

A) The teaching assistant told the pupils to use these crayons to decorate their masks.

B) The teaching assistant told the pupils to use them crayons to decorate their masks.

C) The teaching assistant told the pupils to use that crayons to decorate their masks.

D) The teaching assistant told the pupils to use there crayons to decorate their masks.

16

A) Maths and science is his strongest subject, although he also has an aptitude for languages.

B) Maths and science are his strongest subjects, although he also has an aptitude for languages.

C) Maths and science are his strongest subject, although he also has an aptitude for languages.

D) Maths and science is his strongest subjects, although he also has an aptitude for languages.

17

A) The teacher to who the award was given has been promoted to deputy head.

B) The teacher who the award was given to has been promoted to deputy head.

C) The teacher to whom the award was given has been promoted to deputy head.

D) The teacher whom was given the award has been promoted to deputy head.

Review your answers to practice test 6

1

A) *If the OFSTED inspectors do not see an improvement when they return to the school, the head will have to resign.* The use of the future tense needs to be consistent throughout the sentence. Option A, which states *the head will have to resign,* is the only sentence that matches this phrase correctly with the future need to see an improvement.

2

D) *Child development as a field of study covers all kinds of subjects.* In the sentence the plural word *kinds* needs to agree with the plural word *subjects.*

3

C) *Considering how much revision the student did, her exam results should have been better.* Modal verbs (e.g. *might, should*) must be followed by *have,* rather than *of.* Thus option C is the correct answer because the word *should* is followed by *have.*

4

B) *We were preparing for the Christmas concert when the fire alarm went off.* The plural pronoun *we* must be followed by the plural form of the verb in order for the sentence to agree. Sentence B is the only option where these match.

5

D) *When the next academic year starts, there will be many new pupils who will each learn the school rules.* This is an example of three of the options (A, B and C) using inconsistent tenses following the use of the future tense in the first phrase of the sentence, whereas option D uses the appropriate form of the future tense throughout the sentence.

6

B) *There are many books that pupils can take out of the library but they're not allowed to take them out for more than two weeks at a time. They're/their/there* are very commonly misused. *They're* is correct here because it is a contraction of *they are.*

7

D) *The teacher showed me the solution to the maths problem.* The pronoun *me* is correct when it is the object of the sentence, as in option D. However *me* can't be used as the subject of a sentence, which is why 'Me and the teacher looked over …' is incorrect.

8

C) *Children must remember to wear their plimsolls when they have PE classes. Children* is in the third person, so the correct grammar is for the possessive pronoun –i.e. *their* – to also be in the third person.

9

A) *He and I are presenting a paper at a national teachers' conference next week. He* and *I* are the subjects of the sentence, so the correct grammar in this case is to use *I* as the correct form of the pronoun. This is only found in option A.

10

B) *Peter was the elder of the two brothers.* The comparative form of a word (*elder, wiser, taller*) is used when only two examples are being compared.

11

A) *Every sort of book is available on how to raise your child.* This is the only sentence where the determiner (*every*), the singular subject (*sort*) and singular verb (*is*) agree. The other three options include other determiners (*all, each*) that are inconsistent with either their subject (*sort, sorts*) or their verb (*is, are*).

12

C) *Of all the swimmers on the team this year, Alex is the fastest.* The superlative form of a word (i.e. *fastest, biggest, oldest*) is used when three or more examples are being compared. In this case *all the swimmers* requires the superlative *fastest.*

13

C) *It was the new teacher's stricter regime that the parents preferred.* Option C is the only sentence containing the correct use of grammar. It uses the correct relative pronoun (i.e. *that*) when referring to what the parents preferred. The words *whom* and *who* are not used for objects (i.e. the strict regime) – only for referring to specific people.

14

B) *After raising enough money at the summer fair, the PTA purchased new computer software.* This is the only grammatically correct sentence, as all the other options feature dangling participles. It was the PTA that raised the money at the summer fair, not the new computer software!

15

A) *The teaching assistant told the pupils to use these crayons to decorate their masks.* The answer is the only sentence in which the correct determiner is used – i.e. *these crayons.*

16

B) *Maths and science are his strongest subjects, although he also has an aptitude for languages.* The subject of the sentence is plural – maths *and* science – so the verb needs to be plural (*are*, instead of *is*).

17

C) *The teacher to whom the award was given has been promoted to deputy head.* A handy rule for deciding when to use *who* or *whom* is to substitute *he* or *him* into the sentence. *He* becomes *who*; *him* becomes *whom*. For example: The award was given to *him*. Thus, the teacher *to whom* the award was given.

CHAPTER 7

Reading comprehension tests

The practice tests in this chapter use a passage-based format, where you read a short text and answer related questions. These are mid-level verbal reasoning tests, and mirror the difficulty level of the tests that graduates applying for entry-level or junior managerial positions within the retail or service industries will encounter. You may also take this type of test when applying for a promotion, or as part of a career development programme.

Are you wondering why you need to take a verbal reasoning test if you've already achieved a degree or proven yourself in a business environment? As the number of graduates has risen, employers have turned to verbal reasoning tests to distinguish between large numbers of highly qualified applicants and ensure that they only appoint the most promising individuals.

Instructions

The practice questions in this chapter are in sets of five questions. Read the passage of text and then decide whether the statements that follow are true or false, based only on the information provided in the passage. You should allow yourself six minutes to complete each set of five questions. Once you've completed the practice test, check your answers against the answer explanations that follow the test. Be sure to cover the answers up while you are taking the test!

brilliant tip

Aim to read the passage quickly once, and then more carefully a second time.

Practice test 1

TRUE	FALSE
Answer **TRUE** if the statement is true or follows on logically from the passage.	Answer **FALSE** if the statement is false based ONLY on information in the passage.

The frequency of MRSA being given as the cause of death on death certificates has been increasing significantly for several years. MRSA is an infection-causing bacterium that has developed a resistance to penicillin and many other antibiotics. MRSA infections represent a particular danger for hospital patients with weakened immune systems or open wounds. Scientific trials are testing whether MRSA develops resistance after exposure to new drugs. A research breakthrough would herald a cure for the MRSA threat.

1) MRSA is resistant to all antibiotics.
   TRUE/ FALSE

2) MRSA-related deaths are now more common.
   TRUE/ FALSE

3) Further research is being conducted to study MRSA.
   TRUE/ FALSE

4) Penicillin is an effective treatment for MRSA.
   TRUE/ FALSE

5) MRSA can prove fatal.
   TRUE/ FALSE

Review your answers to practice test 1

1) FALSE. The passage does not say that MRSA is resistant to *all* antibiotics, only *to penicillin and many other antibiotics*. *Many* is **not** the same as *all*.

2) TRUE. The passage states that *The frequency of MRSA being given as the cause of death on death certificates has been **increasing significantly** for several years.*

3) TRUE. The last two sentences state that *Scientific trials are testing whether MRSA develops resistance after exposure to new drugs. A research breakthrough would herald a cure for the MRSA threat.* Scientific trials are a form of research.

4) FALSE. The passage refers to MRSA having *developed a resistance to penicillin*. This means that penicillin is **not** an effective treatment.

5) TRUE. The passage refers to MRSA as a cause of death, so it can indeed be fatal.

Practice test 2

TRUE	FALSE
Answer **TRUE** if the statement is true or follows on logically from the passage.	Answer **FALSE** if the statement is false based ONLY on information in the passage.

The Large Hadron Collider (LHC), located underneath the border of France and Switzerland, is currently the biggest experiment in the world. Its construction involved 9,000 magnets and over 10,000 tons of nitrogen are used for its cooling processes. Scientists and engineers have spent £4.5 billion on building an underground track at CERN, the world's largest particle physics laboratory. This enormous scientific instrument will collect a huge amount of data, but only a small percentage of what is recorded will be useful. When proton atoms – travelling almost at light speed – collide inside the LHC, theoretical physicists expect new forces and particles to be produced. It may even be possible to study black holes using this experiment.

1) Protons travel around the LHC at light speed.
   TRUE/ FALSE

2) The cost of the LHC's track was over £4.5 billion.
   TRUE/ FALSE

3) The LHC is the largest experiment ever conducted in Europe.
   TRUE/ FALSE

4) The LHC was designed to study black holes.
   TRUE/ FALSE

5) The LHC uses over 10,000 tons of oxygen for its cooling processes.
   TRUE/ FALSE

Review your answers to practice test 2

1) FALSE. The passage states *almost at light speed*. The expression 'almost, but not quite' applies here – *almost* the speed of light is not quite as fast as the actual speed of light.

2) FALSE. The passage cites the *exact* cost of £4.5 billion.

3) TRUE. The passage states that the LHC *is currently the biggest experiment in the world*. Since Europe is part of the world, it follows that the LHC is also the largest experiment in Europe.

4) FALSE. The passage states that it may even be possible to study black holes using this experiment; however, this was not the reason why the LHC was designed.

5) FALSE. The passage states that *over 10,000 tons of **nitrogen** are used for its cooling processes.* It is important to read every word of the question. Don't get caught out on easy questions by reading them too quickly.

Practice test 3

TRUE	FALSE
Answer **TRUE** if the statement is true or follows on logically from the passage.	Answer **FALSE** if the statement is false based ONLY on information in the passage.

Critics of modern quasi-non-governmental organisations point to their remoteness, lack of accountability and the difficulty of managing such bureaucratic organisations. Quangos, which are funded by the government but operate at an arm's length, are often viewed by the public as inefficient and ineffective, spending more time talking about their goals than actually achieving them. Controversial though they may be, there is evidence of a rise in the number of quangos in the UK, though many of these state-run organisations use alternative names such as executive agency, board, council or commission. A recent report that the UK's quangos spent over one billion pounds last year on public relations and communications is not likely to improve these organisations' popularity with taxpayers.

1) Modern quangos are entirely independent from government.
   TRUE/ FALSE

2) Quangos are funded by the taxpayer.
   TRUE/ FALSE

3) The public perceive quangos as inefficient because of their marketing spend.
   TRUE/ FALSE

4) The passage suggests that quangos are bureaucratic.
   TRUE/ FALSE

5) The terms executive agency and quango are interchangeable.
   TRUE/ FALSE

Review your answers to practice test 3

1)   FALSE. The passage refers to: *Quangos, which … operate at an arm's length [from the government]*. The question hinges on what is meant by operating at arm's length, which is that whilst there is some independent control, it is not completely independent. Similarly, the word 'quasi' is very important – it means 'apparently, but not really', so while a quango may appear independent, it is not.

2)   TRUE. This can be logically deduced from the passage's last sentence, which tells us that quangos are not popular with taxpayers. Similarly, the second sentence states that quangos are *funded by the government* (i.e. with funds raised from taxes).

3)   FALSE. The passage suggests that the public perceives quangos as inefficient, because of their inefficiency and lack of tangible results. While the last sentence mentions high spending on PR and communication, it cites a recent report, whereas quangos' unpopularity already exists so cannot be caused by this.

4)   TRUE. The passage states that: *Critics of modern quasi-non-governmental organisations point to their remoteness, lack of accountability and the difficulty of managing such* **bureaucratic organisations**.

5)   TRUE. The passage refers to: *evidence of a rise in the number of quangos in the UK, though many of these state-run organisations use alternative names such as executive agency, board, council or commission.*

Practice test 4

TRUE	FALSE
Answer **TRUE** if the statement is true or follows on logically from the passage.	Answer **FALSE** if the statement is false based ONLY on information in the passage.

Large areas of land are needed for growing plants that will be distilled into biofuels. Producing biofuels from agricultural commodities has forced up the price of food. This is just one of the negative impacts that increased biofuel production has had on food security. In August, food scientist Sharon de Cruz demanded an immediate financial review of the current system of subsidies. Her argument is that there are more cost-efficient ways of supporting biofuels. For example, studies have indicated that genetically modifying crops will improve their suitability for producing biofuels.

1) Sharon de Cruz made a scientific recommendation based on environmental concerns.
   TRUE/ FALSE

2) Genetically modified crops produce biofuels more efficiently.
   TRUE/ FALSE

3) Biofuel production requires large amounts of land.
   TRUE/ FALSE

4) Food security is improved by the increased use of biofuels.
   TRUE/ FALSE

5) Subsidies are one way of supporting biofuel production.
   TRUE/ FALSE

Review your answers to practice test 4

1)   FALSE. The passage states: *In August, food scientist Sharon de Cruz demanded an immediate financial review of the current system of subsidies.* Sharon is indeed a scientist, but her recommendation is based on financial reasons rather than environmental concerns.

2)   TRUE. The last sentence states: *studies have indicated that genetically modifying crops will improve their suitability for producing biofuels.*

3)   TRUE. This is explained in the first sentence: *Large areas of land are needed for growing plants that will be distilled into biofuels.*

4)   FALSE. Food security is mentioned in the third sentence: *Producing biofuels from agricultural commodities has forced up the price of food. This is just one of the negative impacts that increased biofuel production has had on food security.* The passage considers there to be a negative impact, rather than an improvement in food security.

5)   TRUE. The relevant parts of the passage are as follows: *In August, food scientist Sharon de Cruz demanded an immediate financial review of the current system of subsidies. Her argument is that there are more cost-efficient ways of supporting biofuels.* In other words, one way of supporting biofuels is by subsidy.

Practice test 5

TRUE	FALSE
Answer **TRUE** if the statement is true or follows on logically from the passage.	Answer **FALSE** if the statement is false based ONLY on information in the passage.

There are now several million cars in the UK using satellite navigation (satnav) systems. These increasingly popular satnav systems mean that motorists no longer have to read maps while they are driving. There are two other major advantages: reduced journey time and reduced mileage (and thus fuel consumption) on unfamiliar routes. System improvements have made these devices much more accurate than earlier models, and today's designs are easier to use and have fewer distracting features. Although some safety surveys highlight the dangers of operating dashboard devices while driving, research conducted by one satnav manufacturer showed that nearly 70 per cent of drivers felt calmer and more focused on the road when using a satnav system.

1) Most drivers feel calmer when using a satnav system.
    TRUE/ FALSE

2) Controversy remains about the effects that satnav systems have on driver concentration.
    TRUE/ FALSE

3) Satellite navigation systems are useful for those people who can't read maps.
    TRUE/ FALSE

4) The passage suggests that a satnav system can make navigation more efficient.
    TRUE/ FALSE

5) Early satnav systems were less accurate than modern ones.
    TRUE/ FALSE

Review your answers to practice test 5

1) TRUE. The passage states: *research ...showed that nearly 70 per cent of drivers felt calmer and more focused on the road when using a satnav system.* The figure of 70 per cent is a clear majority, and therefore the term 'most' is accurate.

2) TRUE. The passage explains that *Although some safety surveys highlight the dangers of operating dashboard devices while driving, research ...showed that nearly 70 per cent of drivers felt calmer and more focused on the road when using a satnav system.* These two contradictory pieces of research indicate that there is controversy over satnavs and safety.

3) TRUE. This follows logically from the second sentence: *motorists no longer have to read maps while they are driving.* If map reading is no longer required, it will, of course, be easier for people who cannot read them!

4) TRUE. The passage states: *There are two other major advantages: reduced journey time and reduced mileage (and thus fuel consumption) on unfamiliar routes.* This means that there are both time and fuel efficiencies.

5) TRUE. The fourth sentence reads: *System improvements have made these devices much **more accurate** than earlier models.* If satnav systems are more accurate now, it follows that they were less accurate in the past.

Practice test 6

TRUE	FALSE
Answer **TRUE** if the statement is true or follows on logically from the passage.	Answer **FALSE** if the statement is false based ONLY on information in the passage.

Peru's Machu Picchu has been a popular tourist destination since it was discovered in 1911. These mountain-top ruins have become one of the most famous symbols of the Incan empire. The difficult terrain surrounding Machu Picchu meant that Spanish conquistadors never discovered the city. It has been theorised, given the virtual inaccessibility of the site, that it was built for religious – rather than economic or military – reasons. This UNESCO World Heritage Site's 200 buildings include many temples and houses. The construction of these buildings relied upon using many perfectly fitting granite blocks without the use of mortar.

1) Machu Picchu is known to have been a religious centre.
   TRUE/ FALSE

2) Machu Picchu is a ruined city in Peru.
   TRUE/ FALSE

3) Machu Picchu was built in 1911.
   TRUE/ FALSE

4) Its valley location protected Machu Picchu from the Spanish conquistadors.
   TRUE/ FALSE

5) Skilled stonemasons were involved in Machu Picchu's construction.
   TRUE/ FALSE

Review your answers to practice test 6

1) FALSE. The passage states: *it has been theorised, given the virtual inaccessibility of the site, that it was built for religious – rather than economic or military – reasons.* In other words there are different theories – none of which have been proved – about the purpose of Machu Picchu.

2) TRUE. The first sentence refers to *Peru's Machu Picchu*, thus confirming the location. The second sentence refers to *mountain-top ruins*, establishing that it is ruined. The third sentence says that … *Spanish conquistadors never discovered the city*, confirming that Machu Picchu is indeed a city. Sometimes the information you need to answer correctly is found in more than one sentence.

3) FALSE. The passage states that it was *discovered in 1911*. The second sentence calls Machu Picchu *one of the most famous symbols of the Incan Empire*, establishing that the city was built long before 1911.

4) FALSE. The second and third sentences mention *mountain-top ruins* and *difficult terrain* respectively. Thus while it is true that it was the terrain that protected Machu Picchu from invaders, it was not located in a valley.

5) TRUE. The passage mentions that the *[buildings were constructed] using perfectly fitting granite blocks without the use of mortar.* It therefore logically follows that skilled stonemasons were involved.

Practice test 7

TRUE	FALSE
Answer **TRUE** if the statement is true or follows on logically from the passage.	Answer **FALSE** if the statement is false based ONLY on information in the passage.

Over the last ten years the reach and the sophistication of international supply chains has increased. The three main factors influencing global supply chain design are manufacturing operations, distribution and transportation. These logistic networks connect the supplier's base to its end customer goods and services. There are always several companies seeking to maximise their own profits in any single global supply chain. But it is in the interest of each company in the chain to deal with the others fairly, as their mutual success depends on every link in the chain operating efficiently. Failure can also be shared. A supplier experiencing financial difficulties can soon pass its credit problems to other companies – even to more profitable organisations – along the lines of their interconnected supply chain. There are practical measures for avoiding such contagion from defaulting suppliers or manufacturers. One such safety net involves building a network of multiple suppliers, multiple production facilities and multiple storage facilities – though this, of course, is not always possible for smaller companies.

1) Every company in a supply chain should try to make the maximum profit.
   TRUE/ FALSE

2) Manufacturing companies who default can spread their credit problems throughout the supply system.
   TRUE/ FALSE

3) International supply chains are planned around only three considerations.
   TRUE/ FALSE

4) The passage suggests that to minimise business risk, it may
    be advisable to have more than one supplier.
    TRUE/ FALSE

5) There is an indiscriminate impact throughout a supply
    chain if a supplier is experiencing credit difficulties.
    TRUE/ FALSE

Review your answers to practice test 7

1) FALSE. While the passage says that *There are always several companies seeking to maximise their own profits in any single global supply chain,* the next sentence says that fair dealing between supply chain companies is essential to success.

2) TRUE. The passage describes how this happens. *A supplier* (i.e. a manufacturing company) *experiencing financial difficulties can soon pass its credit problems to other companies – even to more profitable organisations – along the lines of their interconnected supply chain.*

3) FALSE. The passage describes the three *main* factors, which are: *manufacturing operations, distribution and transportation.* It therefore follows that there are minor considerations in addition to the three main ones – so the word 'only' does not apply.

4) TRUE. The last sentence states that *One such safety net involves building a network of multiple suppliers, multiple production facilities and multiple storage facilities.* A safety net is a way to minimise risk – and here having more than one supplier is given as an example.

5) TRUE. The passage explains that credit problems can be passed to *other companies – even to more profitable companies – along the lines of their interconnected supply chain.* Thus the impact does not discriminate between more and less profitable organisations.

Practice test 8

TRUE	FALSE
Answer **TRUE** if the statement is true or follows on logically from the passage.	Answer **FALSE** if the statement is false based ONLY on information in the passage.

Digital broadcasting heralds a new paradigm in television broadcasting. This sophisticated broadcasting technology allows broadcasters to offer television with multiple broadcasting choices and interactive capabilities and high-quality sound and image. However, digital broadcasting should not be confused with High-Definition Television, which offers the very best audio and picture clarity. Both the UK and the USA have already made the transition from analogue to digital broadcasting. There, television stations have stopped broadcasting along analogue channels, and any viewers with analogue television sets must use special set-top conversion boxes in order to view programmes. As well as benefiting viewers with superior entertainment options, the switch to digital broadcasting frees up part of the valuable broadcasting spectrum that can then be used for public and emergency services.

1)   Digital television offers the best audio and visual quality.
     TRUE/ FALSE

2)   In the USA, analogue televisions can no longer be used.
     TRUE/ FALSE

3)   The switch to digital broadcasting benefits the emergency services.
     TRUE/ FALSE

4)   The UK will soon convert to exclusively digital broadcasting.
     TRUE/ FALSE

5)   A set-top box is necessary in order to access digital broadcasts.
     TRUE/ FALSE

Review your answers to practice test 8

1) FALSE. The passage states that *High-Definition Television* offers the very best audio and picture clarity.

2) FALSE. The passage explains that in the USA (and the UK) analogue televisions can still be used with set-top conversion boxes.

3) TRUE. The passage states that *the switch to digital broadcasting frees up part of the valuable broadcasting spectrum that can then be used for public and emergency services.*

4) FALSE. This conversion has already occurred, as specified in the fourth and fifth sentences.

5) FALSE. A set-top box is only necessary for viewers with analogue televisions.

Practice test 9

TRUE	FALSE
Answer **TRUE** if the statement is true or follows on logically from the passage.	Answer **FALSE** if the statement is false based ONLY on information in the passage.

Wildlife expert Dr Ellen Boyle spoke at this year's Wildlife Conservation Conference about the lack of a strategy to prevent the imminent extinction of a number of primate species across Asia. Her talk focused on the dangers of hunters and the clearing of tropical rainforests across the continent. Several species of Asian monkey, some only recently discovered, are facing these dual threats to their natural habitats. Dr Boyle differentiated the most at-risk primates as critically endangered, but the talk stressed that other species were also living under constant threat. Dr Boyle's scientific paper presented compelling evidence of the need to halt deforestation, but in some developing Asian economies, where wood is collected for fuel and for sale and land is cleared for farming, human interests currently take precedence over the fate of the region's lower-order primates.

1) Dr Boyle's talk at the Wildlife Conservation Conference explained the strategy for protecting Asian primates.
TRUE/ FALSE

2) The passage gives three reasons for the destruction of tropical rainforests.
TRUE/ FALSE

3) All Asian primates are threatened by extinction.
TRUE/ FALSE

4) The deforestation of rainforests is the only threat to Asian primates.
TRUE/ FALSE

5) Dr Boyle suggests that all Asian countries prioritise economics over the survival of monkeys.
TRUE/ FALSE

Review your answers to practice test 9

1) FALSE. While Dr Boyle did speak at the Wildlife Conservation Conference, the first sentence refers to *the lack of a strategy* – so she could not have explained the strategy in her talk.

2) TRUE. The passage describes the following three reasons: (1) collecting wood for fuel, (2) collecting wood for sale and (3) clearing the land for farming. There may well be other factors contributing to deforestation, but the statement specifically referred to those reasons given in the passage.

3) FALSE. The first sentence in the passage refers to the *imminent extinction of **a number of** primate species across Asia*. 'A number of' does not equate to 'all'. Furthermore, later in the passage, Dr Boyle differentiates the most at-risk primates as critically endangered – so it logically follows that other Asian primates are not at such a high level of risk.

4) FALSE. The second sentence mentions the *dangers of hunters*, as well as the clearing of tropical rainforests.

5) FALSE. The last sentence of the passage states that: *in **some developing Asian economies** ... human interests currently take precedence over the fate of the region's lower-order primates*. 'Some' is not the same as 'all'. Dr Boyle's paper specifies that it is not all Asian economies – and not even all of the developing economies – that prioritise financial concerns over those of primates.

Practice test 10

TRUE	FALSE
Answer **TRUE** if the statement is true or follows on logically from the passage.	Answer **FALSE** if the statement is false based ONLY on information in the passage.

Last month the market research company Du Balle Inc. reported that the organic food sector grew over the past year, but not at the same rate as the previous five years during which the market grew fivefold. An oft-asked question about organic food is – why does it cost so much more? The simple answer is that organically grown products cost more to farm than their conventionally produced counterparts. Higher production costs due to methods such as crop rotation, hand-weeding (rather than pesticides) and the use of animal manure (instead of chemical fertilisers) result in higher costs to the consumer. Sceptics claim that organic foods are no healthier than non-organic foods. But proponents of organic farming counter that organically produced foods contain fewer contaminants – and that these health benefits more than justify the price differential. A spokeswoman from the Organic Farming Association said: 'Organic farming is about sustainability – and this means economic sustainability for struggling farmers, as well as sustainable food production.'

1) Growth in the organic food market is slowing.
   TRUE/ FALSE

2) Using animal manure costs more than chemical fertilisers.
   TRUE/ FALSE

3) The health benefits of organically grown food is indisputable.
   TRUE/ FALSE

4) Organically grown food contains no pesticides and contaminants.
   TRUE/ FALSE

5) The organic farming movement has no financial motivation.
   TRUE/ FALSE

Review your answers to practice test 10

1) TRUE. According to the passage's first sentence, *Last month the market research company Du Balle Inc. reported that the organic food* **sector grew over the past year, but not at the same rate as for the previous five years** *during which the market grew fivefold.*

2) TRUE. The passage's third and fourth sentences explain that using organic farming methods, such as animal manure, costs more than conventional ones.

3) FALSE. The passage suggests that there is controversy over the health benefits of organic food – so therefore it cannot be said to be indisputable. *Sceptics claim that organic foods are no healthier than non-organic foods. But proponents of organic farming counter that organically produced foods contain fewer contaminants …*

4) FALSE. The passage states that: *organically produced foods contain fewer contaminants.* 'Fewer' suggests that there are still some contaminants in organically grown food.

5) FALSE. The passage quotes the Organic Farming Association as saying, '*Organic farming is about sustainability – and this means* **economic sustainability** *for struggling farmers, as well as sustainable food production.*' Economic considerations are certainly one of the movement's motivating factors.

Practice test 11

TRUE	FALSE
Answer **TRUE** if the statement is true or follows on logically from the passage.	Answer **FALSE** if the statement is false based ONLY on information in the passage.

The Arctic region around the North Pole lacks specific land boundaries and has alternative definitions, such as its distinctive ecology. The Arctic region's ecosystem is comprised of many species of plant, bird, fish and mammal, including polar bears. There is life above, below and even within this huge ocean of ice. But the natural habitat of these Arctic animals is being threatened by the effects of global warming. Typically, the North Pole's ice cap diminishes in summer and then replenishes itself in the winter months. However, scientists speculate that warmer oceans are causing a dramatic thinning of the Arctic's ice during winter that has resulted in ice-free gaps of ocean in the summer. Some experts predict that the entire ice cap will have disappeared by the end of this century.

1) Marine mammals are the only things living in the Arctic.
   TRUE/ FALSE

2) The Arctic's seasonal pattern is to reduce in size during the winter months.
   TRUE/ FALSE

3) One theory is that higher seawater temperatures are making the Arctic melt.
   TRUE/ FALSE

4) The Arctic has fixed geographic borders.
   TRUE/ FALSE

5) All of the Arctic's ice disappears in the summer.
   TRUE/ FALSE

Review your answers to practice test 11

1)   FALSE. The passage states that *The Arctic region's ecosystem is comprised of many species of plant, bird, fish and mammal, including polar bears.* There are many other living things in the Arctic besides marine mammals.

2)   FALSE. The passage states that the Arctic *replenishes itself in winter months.* It diminishes in the summer, not the winter.

3)   TRUE. The passage states that *scientists speculate that warmer oceans are causing a dramatic thinning of the Arctic's ice.* The statement is simply expressing this idea in different words.

4)   FALSE. The passage says: *The Arctic region around the North Pole **lacks specific land boundaries** ...*

5)   FALSE. The passage mentions *ice-free gaps of ocean in the summer.* But it does not say that *all* of the ice melts.

Practice test 12

TRUE	FALSE
Answer **TRUE** if the statement is true or follows on logically from the passage.	Answer **FALSE** if the statement is false based ONLY on information in the passage.

Ethical labels are now widely used on products, such as coffee, to show that the goods in question have been produced in a worker-friendly manner. A ban on child workers is one labour practice to which ethically labelled suppliers must strictly adhere. Despite increased public awareness, many UK retail stores may still be selling products produced by foreign workers paid extremely low wages. Although working conditions have improved in some companies as a result of labelling, sweatshop wages and a lack of union representation remain prevalent in other suppliers from developing countries. There is also a danger that, where ethical codes of practice have been implemented, the supply workers themselves are inadvertently punished with lower pay.

1) Unions are widespread in developing countries.
   TRUE/ FALSE

2) The use of ethical labelling has not improved working conditions.
   TRUE/ FALSE

3) Ethical labelling is still quite rare in UK retail stores.
   TRUE/ FALSE

4) Ethically labelled coffee cannot have been harvested by children.
   TRUE/ FALSE

5) The passage suggests that using ethical labels on products can have both a beneficial and a detrimental effect.
   TRUE/ FALSE

Review your answers to practice test 12

1) FALSE. The passage notes: *a **lack of union represen-tation** remain[s] prevalent in other suppliers from developing countries.* Unions cannot be widespread if there is a lack of them.

2) FALSE. The passage states that *working conditions have improved in some companies as a result of labelling.* Some improvement has been made, so the answer is false.

3) FALSE. The passage states that *Ethical labels are now **widely used**.* If they are widely used, the practice is not rare.

4) TRUE. You must apply logic to the passage to answer this question. The second sentence states: *A ban on child workers is one labour practice to which ethically labelled suppliers must strictly adhere.* So although coffee harvesting is not specifically discussed, it follows that coffee cannot have been harvested by children if it is ethically labelled.

5) TRUE. The passage refers to an improvement: *Although working conditions have improved in some companies as a result of labelling ...* but also states: *There is also a danger that, where ethical codes of practice have been implemented, the supply workers themselves are inadvertently punished with lower pay.*

Practice test 13

TRUE	FALSE
Answer **TRUE** if the statement is true or follows on logically from the passage.	Answer **FALSE** if the statement is false based ONLY on information in the passage.

The UK has a target of cutting its carbon emissions by using renewable sources to generate a third of its electricity by 2020. One option is to invest heavily in building thousands of wind farms around the country. But a key technological issue that remains to be solved is how to efficiently store wind-powered electricity so as to ensure the regularity of supply that is needed by consumers. Other solutions for cutting carbon emissions are to increase the amount of the electricity supplied by nuclear power or to build more coal-fired power stations equipped with carbon capture technology that reduces greenhouse gas emissions by capturing and storing carbon dioxide.

1) Wind-powered electricity needs to be stored before being distributed to consumers.
   TRUE/ FALSE

2) The passage suggests that carbon capture technology reduces carbon dioxide emissions from coal-fired power stations.
   TRUE/ FALSE

3) The UK has a target of cutting its carbon emissions by a third by 2020.
   TRUE/ FALSE

4) Wind farms are a renewable source of energy.
   TRUE/ FALSE

5) The passage proposes nuclear power as an alternative to electricity.
   TRUE/ FALSE

Review your answers to practice test 13

1) TRUE. The passage explains, when discussing wind energy, that there is a need *to efficiently store wind-powered electricity so as to ensure the regularity of supply that is needed by consumers.*

2) TRUE. The last sentence explains that *Other solutions … are to … build more coal-fired power stations equipped with carbon capture technology that reduces greenhouse gas emissions by capturing and storing carbon dioxide.* In other words, the technology stores carbon dioxide rather than releasing it as emissions.

3) FALSE. The UK does indeed have a 2020 target, but it is to generate a third of its electricity using renewable sources. This involves cutting carbon emissions, but it does not necessarily mean cutting them by a third.

4) TRUE. The second sentence refers to wind farming as an option for reaching the renewable energy target.

5) FALSE. The passage says: *Other solutions for cutting carbon emissions are to increase the amount of the electricity supplied by nuclear power …* Nuclear power is suggested as an alternative means of supplying electricity, rather than a substitute for electricity itself.

Practice test 14

TRUE	FALSE
Answer **TRUE** if the statement is true or follows on logically from the passage.	Answer **FALSE** if the statement is false based ONLY on information in the passage.

There are several thousand patients waiting for organ transplants in the UK. This urgent need has led to a government review of how best to increase organ donation rates. The introduction of presumed consent – as found in other European countries – has now been put forward as a possible solution. Such a drastic and controversial change, whereby donating organs would become the default option, would require a new legal framework. Among many other proposals, the government's review recommended establishing the following: locally adapted national policies for organ donation; a best practice framework; and a national organisation to coordinate transplants.

1) Presumed consent means that donating your bodily organs is the standard option.
   TRUE/ FALSE

2) Implementing presumed consent would necessitate new legislation.
   TRUE/ FALSE

3) The number of patients waiting for transplants led to the government's review of the current situation.
   TRUE/ FALSE

4) One recommendation was to introduce a standard national policy for all hospitals.
   TRUE/ FALSE

5) Presumed consent was not proposed in the government's recommendations because it lacks popular support.
   TRUE/ FALSE

Review your answers to practice test 14

1) TRUE. The passage explains that a switch to presumed consent would be a drastic change. Currently, the default option is to *not* donate your organs. But under presumed consent *donating organs would become the default option.*

2) TRUE. The fourth sentence explains that to introduce presumed consent *would require a new legal framework.*

3) TRUE. The passage states: *There are several thousand patients waiting for organ transplants in the UK. This urgent need has led to a government review ...*

4) FALSE. The relevant part of the passage reads as follows: *the government's review recommended establishing the following:* **locally adapted national policies** *for organ donation ...* While a new national policy for organ donation has been recommended, the passage provides further stipulation that the policies are to be adapted for local use.

5) FALSE. The passage acknowledges that the introduction of presumed consent would be controversial, but it also states that it has been put forward as a possible solution as part of the government review regardless.

CHAPTER 8

Verbal reasoning tests

A s with the practice tests in Chapter 7, the tests in this chapter feature a passage-based format. The main difference is that the tests in this chapter are more advanced, in terms of the subject matter and language used in the passages. Although the texts are not necessarily longer than those in the previous chapter, answering the questions will involve a greater degree of verbal reasoning. In addition to 'true' and 'false', the tests that follow introduce a third answer option: 'cannot tell'.

These advanced verbal reasoning tests mirror the difficulty level of tests that graduates applying for accelerated promotion schemes in banking, management consultancy or the public sector will encounter. Passages will typically be set in a financial or business context related to the role being applied for. The practice tests in this chapter are also at an equivalent level of difficulty to the UKCAT's verbal reasoning test, which is taken by applicants to British medical and dental schools.

Instructions

The practice questions in this chapter are in sets of five questions. Read the passage of text and then decide whether the statements that follow are true or false, based only on the information provided in the passage. You should allow yourself six minutes to complete each set of five questions. Once you've completed the practice test, check your answers against the answer explanations that follow the test. Be sure to cover the answers up while you are taking the test!

brilliant tip

When doing this sort of test you need to differentiate between shades of grey. Remember that your objectivity is being tested, so do not allow your personal opinions or outside knowledge to influence how you answer.

Practice test 1

TRUE	FALSE	CANNOT TELL
Answer **TRUE** if the statement is true or follows on logically from the passage.	Answer **FALSE** if the statement is false based ONLY on information in the passage.	Answer **CANNOT TELL** if there is insufficient information given in the passage.

For small to medium-sized businesses, outsourcing payroll operations is almost certainly a way to save time and staff costs. Payroll-service providers utilise specially designed computer systems, resulting in greater speed, accuracy and flexibility than an in-house department. Outsourcing the time-consuming burden of payroll administration enables businesses to be more focused and productive. However, organisations that outsource their payroll functions should remember that employers are ultimately accountable for the payment of their employees' income taxes and national insurance payments – and should thus choose their provider wisely.

1) Large businesses would not benefit from outsourcing payroll operations.
   TRUE/ FALSE/ CANNOT TELL

2) Fraudulent payroll-service providers can be held responsible for an employer's non-payment of taxes.
   TRUE/ FALSE/ CANNOT TELL

3) One possible benefit of outsourcing payroll operations is reduced employee overheads.
   TRUE/ FALSE/ CANNOT TELL

4) The passage states that small businesses can always save money by outsourcing payroll functions.
   TRUE/ FALSE/ CANNOT TELL

5) The passage suggests that payroll-service providers will make fewer mistakes than in-house payroll staff.
   TRUE/ FALSE/ CANNOT TELL

Review your answers to practice test 1

1) CANNOT TELL. The first sentence of the passage establishes that the piece is focusing on *small to medium-sized businesses.* Whilst there is no specific mention of large businesses, there is also nothing in the passage to suggest that the benefits described could not also apply to large businesses.

2) FALSE. The relevant part of the passage states that *organisations that outsource their payroll functions should remember that employers are ultimately accountable for the payment of their employees' income taxes and national insurance payments.* In other words the employers – and not payroll-service providers – remain responsible.

3) TRUE. In the words of the passage: *For small to medium-sized businesses, outsourcing payroll operations is almost certainly a way to save time and staff costs.* This means that employee overheads (i.e. staff costs) can be reduced by outsourcing payroll operations.

4) FALSE. In the first sentence, the passage states: *For small to medium-sized businesses, outsourcing payroll operations is **almost certainly** a way to save time and staff costs. Almost certainly* is not the same thing as *always.* Whereas *always* is an absolute, *almost certainly* suggests that there may be some exceptions to the rule. So it is false to say that businesses can always save money by outsourcing payroll functions.

5) TRUE. One of the points made by the passage is the improved accuracy (*resulting in greater speed, **accuracy** and flexibility*) that payroll-service providers can bring. Greater accuracy equates to fewer mistakes, and thus the statement is true.

Practice test 2

TRUE	FALSE	CANNOT TELL
Answer **TRUE** if the statement is true or follows on logically from the passage.	Answer **FALSE** if the statement is false based ONLY on information in the passage.	Answer **CANNOT TELL** if there is insufficient information given in the passage.

Conglomerate Plc, which supplies over twenty thousand products to retailers in 50 countries and purchases parts from 312 factories, has one of the world's most sophisticated supply chains. This close collaboration with suppliers adds value to its business and reaps commercial advantage. At the same time Conglomerate Plc prides itself on considering the macro-economic impact of social and environmental factors in its dealings with supply chain partners. Although Conglomerate Plc's ultra-efficient supply chain benefits consumers by lowering retail prices, critics of this manufacturing giant maintain that the constant pressure on its suppliers to cut costs has a negative impact on workers' pay and benefits.

1) Conglomerate Plc prioritises the environment in its negotiations with suppliers.
    TRUE/ FALSE/ CANNOT TELL

2) The passage suggests that global supply chains are of universal benefit.
    TRUE/ FALSE/ CANNOT TELL

3) Conglomerate Plc operates in more than 50 countries and has 312 factories.
    TRUE/ FALSE/ CANNOT TELL

4) Conglomerate Plc does not sell its products direct to the consumer.
    TRUE/ FALSE/ CANNOT TELL

5) Conglomerate Plc has unpredictable delivery systems.
    TRUE/ FALSE/ CANNOT TELL

Review your answers to practice test 2

1) CANNOT TELL. The passage states that Conglomerate Plc ... *prides itself on considering the macro-economic impact of social and environmental factors, in its dealings with supply chain partners.* However, it cannot be ascertained from the passage how much emphasis or importance environmental concerns are given when weighed up against other factors.

2) FALSE. The reason that this statement is false is that the passage refers to the *negative impact on workers' pay and benefits.* Global supply chains cannot be said to be universally beneficial if there are some exceptions to the rule (i.e. poorly paid workers).

3) FALSE. The relevant part of the passage states that *Conglomerate Plc ... supplies over twenty thousand products to retailers in 50 countries and purchases parts from 312 factories.* This question highlights the importance of paying careful attention to each word in the question – in particular key words, such as *more than.* Conglomerate Plc only operates in 50 countries. No more. Furthermore, it does not have 312 factories; rather, it *purchases parts* from 312 factories.

4) CANNOT TELL. The passage states that Conglomerate Plc sells to retailers, but there is no way of telling whether or not the organisation also sells direct to customers. You may think this is likely and be tempted to answer FALSE. But remember you must base your answer on the information provided in the passage, and there is simply not enough to give a conclusive answer.

5) FALSE. The passage refers to the *ultra-efficient supply chain* so it follows that its delivery systems would be predictable, rather than unpredictable.

Practice test 3

TRUE	FALSE	CANNOT TELL
Answer **TRUE** if the statement is true or follows on logically from the passage.	Answer **FALSE** if the statement is false based ONLY on information in the passage.	Answer **CANNOT TELL** if there is insufficient information given in the passage.

According to recently published figures, internet sales last year comprised nearly five per cent of the UK's retail spending. It was the only retail channel showing growth, with a 20 per cent rise on the previous year's sales. The flourishing of e-commerce can be largely attributed to the increasing popularity of on-line supermarket shopping and shoppers' preference for staying home. The UK leads its European neighbours in internet shopping revenue, in part because of higher credit card usage than countries such as Germany and France. Compared with continental Europe, the UK also has higher levels of computer ownership and wider access to the broadband services that facilitate internet purchases. Business experts forecast a trebling of internet retail sales in the UK and France over the next five years.

1) Sales trends for internet shopping in Germany have mirrored those in the UK.
   TRUE/ FALSE/ CANNOT TELL

2) The UK is at the forefront of increasing European internet sales.
   TRUE/ FALSE/ CANNOT TELL

3) The passage suggests that internet shopping appeals to consumers who do not like going out to shop at shopping centres.
   TRUE/ FALSE/ CANNOT TELL

4) Low credit card usage is the main reason that continental European countries lag behind the UK in internet retail.
TRUE/ FALSE/ CANNOT TELL

5) Internet retail sales in the UK and France will be higher next year.
TRUE/ FALSE/ CANNOT TELL

Review your answers to practice test 3

1) FALSE. There are a couple of sentences in the passage that refer to Europe, although only one of these refers to Germany specifically: *The UK leads its European neighbours in internet shopping revenue, in part because of higher credit card usage than countries such as Germany and France. Compared with continental Europe, the UK also has higher levels of computer ownership and wider access to the broadband services that facilitate internet purchases.* This information indicates that the UK is showing different internet shopping trends than continental European countries, such as Germany. Hence it is false to say that the two countries are mirroring each other, as they are different rather than similar.

2) TRUE. The key phrase in the passage is: *The UK leads its European neighbours in internet shopping.* The word *leads* tells you that the UK is at the *forefront* of increasing European internet sales.

3) TRUE. In the third sentence, the passage attributes the *flourishing of e-commerce* to shoppers' preference for staying at home

4) CANNOT TELL. This is a tricky question. Low credit card usage is indeed cited as one of the reasons European countries have lower levels of internet shopping. *The UK leads its European neighbours in internet shopping, **in part** because of higher credit card usage.* However, it is not clear whether this is the main factor, as no comparison between the different contributing factors is given.

5) CANNOT TELL. Another tricky question. The statement is making a prediction. The passage also makes a prediction about the future of internet retail sales: *Business experts forecast a trebling of internet retail sales in the UK and France over the next five years.* A forecast for the next five years does

not necessarily mean that the growth will come in the next year, although this is likely. Where the future is concerned, there is no way of knowing whether a prediction is true or not until it actually happens!

Practice test 4

TRUE	FALSE	CANNOT TELL
Answer **TRUE** if the statement is true or follows on logically from the passage.	Answer **FALSE** if the statement is false based ONLY on information in the passage.	Answer **CANNOT TELL** if there is insufficient information given in the passage.

The Board of Directors of Fone Industries (together with its subsidiaries) wishes to inform shareholders in the Company, as well as potential investors, that the consolidated net profit of the Group for the current quarter is expected to show a significant decline as compared to that for the previous quarter. We attribute this unprecedented fall to the global economic downturn that has resulted in a drastic reduction in consumer spending on telecommunication products – and mobile handsets in particular. Fone Industries believes that our diverse, award-winning product portfolio, respected brand and competitive pricing will enable us to weather the current economic situation. The information contained in this announcement is a preliminary assessment; full results for the year will be disclosed in the annual report to be published in April.

1) The global economy has been in recession for the past two quarters.
    TRUE/ FALSE/ CANNOT TELL

2) Fone Industries has suffered a nosedive in profits and is now operating at a loss.
    TRUE/ FALSE/ CANNOT TELL

3) Fone Industries' profits for the current quarter are predicted to be lower than those of the previous quarter.
    TRUE/ FALSE/ CANNOT TELL

4) Fone Industries is paying the price for the poor quality of its mobile phone handsets.
    TRUE/ FALSE/ CANNOT TELL

5)   A worldwide economic recession has negatively impacted
     retail sales of telephones.
     TRUE/ FALSE/ CANNOT TELL

Review your answers to practice test 4

1) CANNOT TELL. The passage makes it clear that there is a *global economic downturn*. It also states that Fone Industries has experienced a downturn for one quarter. However, based on this information, there is no way of working out how long the global economic downturn has been going on.

2) FALSE. The passage refers to a slowdown in profits rather than operating at a loss.

3) TRUE. The passage states that *the consolidated net profit of the Group for the current quarter is expected to show **a significant decline as compared to that for the previous quarter***.

4) FALSE. The answer is FALSE since the passage describes only economic reasons for the fall in profits: *We attribute this unprecedented fall to the global economic downturn*. There is no mention of poor quality products. In fact, Fone Industries' *award-winning product portfolio* and *respected brand* is mentioned, so it follows that products are of high, rather than low, quality.

5) TRUE. The relevant part of the passage is: *We attribute this unprecedented fall to the global economic downturn that has resulted in a drastic reduction in consumer spending on telecommunication products – **and mobile handsets in particular***. Retail sales of telephones have reduced, so the recession has indeed had a negative impact.

Practice test 5

TRUE	FALSE	CANNOT TELL
Answer **TRUE** if the statement is true or follows on logically from the passage.	Answer **FALSE** if the statement is false based ONLY on information in the passage.	Answer **CANNOT TELL** if there is insufficient information given in the passage.

According to the Business School Admission Council, last year applications for full-time MBA programmes declined at 75 per cent of educational institutions offering the degree, with applications down by more than 20 per cent at over half of the schools surveyed. MBAs have traditionally been seen as a fast-track to higher salaries and senior management positions, but the proliferation of MBA programmes has raised questions about the value of the degree. Business schools argue that they offer essential management training, and point to a poll of recent MBA graduates, over 80 per cent of whom rated their programmes as 'excellent'. But critics remain unconvinced that MBAs remain a necessary qualification for a high-power career. Chris Wilson, Senior Partner at Wilson Recruitment & Selection, says: 'An MBA, even from a top-tier school, is no substitute for experience and a successful performance record.' Given the expense of full-time programmes, it is perhaps unsurprising that application figures for part-time executive MBA programmes increased by 50 per cent last year.

1) The passage suggests that the MBA degree has been undermined by the plethora of programmes on offer.
   TRUE/ FALSE/ CANNOT TELL

2) Last year, part-time MBA programmes received more applications than traditional full-time courses.
   TRUE/ FALSE/ CANNOT TELL

3) The quality of MBA courses has declined as the number of programmes on offer has increased.
   TRUE/ FALSE/ CANNOT TELL

4) The passage argues that there is no longer any value in attaining an MBA.
    TRUE/ FALSE/ CANNOT TELL

5) The passage suggests that historically MBAs were used to build a high-powered career.
    TRUE/ FALSE/ CANNOT TELL

Review your answers to practice test 5

1) TRUE. The relevant part of the passage states that *the pro-liferation of MBA programmes has raised questions about the value of the degree.* You might have considered answering CANNOT TELL, as whether or not the MBA degree has been undermined is clearly a matter of ongoing debate. If the statement had read, 'The MBA degree has been under-mined by the plethora of programmes on offer' the answer would indeed have been CANNOT TELL. However, you are asked to determine whether or not **the passage** makes this suggestion. And as it does, the answer is true.

2) CANNOT TELL. The passage states that *last year applica-tions for full-time MBA programmes declined at 75 per cent of educational institutions offering the degree, with applications down by more than 20 per cent at over half of the schools sur-veyed.* So the number of applications for full-time MBAs has reduced. The passage also explains that: *Given the expense of full-time programmes, it is perhaps unsurprising that application figures for part-time executive MBA programmes increased by 50 per cent last year.* We also know that part-time MBA applications have increased. However, there is no mention of how applications for part-time MBAs compare to applications for full-time ones. Without all the relevant figures it is impossible to give a definitive answer.

3) CANNOT TELL. You might think that this is TRUE or FALSE depending upon which part of the passage you focus on. In fact, there is contradictory evidence. Initially, the passage says that *the proliferation of MBA programmes has raised questions about the value of the degree.* It also cites critics expressing doubts over the necessity of an MBA degree. However, the passage also refers to *a poll of recent MBA graduates, over 80 per cent of whom rated their programmes as 'excellent'.* As both sides of the argument

are presented, it is not possible to determine conclusively whether the quality has in fact declined.

4)   FALSE. The passage provides a balanced perspective – rather than being for or against MBAs. Thus it would be FALSE to say that it argues that there is no longer any value in attaining an MBA.

5)   TRUE. The passage explains that *MBAs have traditionally been seen as a fast-track to higher salaries and senior management positions.* A high-powered career is another way of saying a *fast-track*.

Practice test 6

TRUE	FALSE	CANNOT TELL
Answer **TRUE** if the statement is true or follows on logically from the passage.	Answer **FALSE** if the statement is false based ONLY on information in the passage.	Answer **CANNOT TELL** if there is insufficient information given in the passage.

The average British company uses only 55 per cent of its office space and two-thirds of employees are unhappy with their work environment, according to a survey recently undertaken by the design consultancy Best Desks Ltd. This inefficient use of space equates to over ten billion pounds of waste in London alone. The advent of wireless technology means that employees no longer need to be tied to fixed workstations with wires and cables and can work more flexibly. Trend forecasters predict the following innovations to workspaces over the next decade: more collaborative, open-plan spaces to encourage social networking; reservable mobile workstations; easily interlockable office furniture; and bespoke ambient sound and lighting.

1) Staff productivity would be improved if workspaces were more appealingly designed.
    TRUE/ FALSE/ CANNOT TELL

2) The passage suggests that most British companies should move into smaller premises, thus saving money.
    TRUE/ FALSE/ CANNOT TELL

3) Working environments could be more personalised to suit how individual employees like to work.
    TRUE/ FALSE/ CANNOT TELL

4) Two-thirds of British workers are dissatisfied with their jobs.
    TRUE/ FALSE/ CANNOT TELL

5) Flexible working has been facilitated by the rise of wireless technology.
    TRUE/ FALSE/ CANNOT TELL

Review your answers to practice test 6

1) CANNOT TELL. The passage presents arguments for designing work environments more efficiently. It also makes the point that employees *can work more flexibly*. But the passage does not explicitly state that productivity would be improved – this is conjecture so the answer is CANNOT TELL.

2) FALSE. Don't be misled into thinking that this statement is true by the sentence: *This inefficient use of space equates to over ten billion pounds of waste in London alone*. It does not logically follow that companies should therefore move to smaller premises, and nowhere does the passage suggest this.

3) TRUE. A prediction is made as follows: *Trend forecasters predict the following innovations to workspaces over the next decade: more collaborative, open-plan spaces to encourage social networking; reservable mobile workstations; easily interlockable office furniture.* If the question had said 'working environments **will** be more personalised' the answer would be CANNOT TELL as there is no way to predict the future. However, this question used the conditional 'could' – and indeed, several hypothetical innovations are mentioned in the passage, making the correct answer TRUE.

4) CANNOT TELL. Survey evidence that *two-thirds of employees are unhappy with their work environment* is cited. But the passage does not state that they are unhappy with their jobs. Thus the answer is CANNOT TELL.

5) TRUE. The passage states: *The advent of wireless technology means that employees no longer need to be tied to fixed workstations with wires and cables and can work more flexibly.* The answer is TRUE because flexible working is directly attributed to the rise of wireless technology.

Practice test 7

TRUE	FALSE	CANNOT TELL
Answer **TRUE** if the statement is true or follows on logically from the passage.	Answer **FALSE** if the statement is false based ONLY on information in the passage.	Answer **CANNOT TELL** if there is insufficient information given in the passage.

At a time of tumbling share prices and longer life expectancy, many companies have acute shortfalls in their pension funds. Pension schemes in the UK are protected by a government fund contributed to by companies themselves, but many British business leaders have been lobbying for a change of rules in instances of a company restructuring. A company is currently required to fully cover its pension liabilities when disposing of a division – a rule seen by some as obstructive to corporate activity. In theory, new legislation could allow businesses to transfer their pension liabilities to other divisions. However, critics believe that this could give organisations carte blanche to shift their pension obligations to entities likely to become insolvent, thus forcing other organisations to subsidise their pension commitments.

1) Most British company directors believe that existing pension legislation impedes restructuring.
    TRUE/ FALSE/ CANNOT TELL

2) The passage cites three main reasons for deficits in companies' pension funds.
    TRUE/ FALSE/ CANNOT TELL

3) Current legislation allows British businesses to default on their pension obligations when they restructure.
    TRUE/ FALSE/ CANNOT TELL

4) Controversy surrounds any relaxation of pension rules about restructuring.
    TRUE/ FALSE/ CANNOT TELL

5) A change in pension legislation will help companies to reduce the hole in their pension schemes.
TRUE/ FALSE/ CANNOT TELL

Review your answers to practice test 7

1) CANNOT TELL. The passage states that *many British business leaders have been lobbying for a change of rules in instances of a company restructuring.* Be careful here – 'many' does not mean the same as 'most'. For the term *most* to be accurate, the passage would have to indicate that a majority of business leaders felt that the rules are obstructive. And while many leaders clearly feel this way, there may also be many business leaders who disagree. There is simply no way of knowing.

2) FALSE. Only two reasons are given. These are *tumbling share prices* and *longer life expectancy.*

3) FALSE. The passage states that *A company is currently required to fully cover its pension liabilities when disposing of a division.* So it is not correct to say that British businesses can default on their pension obligations following a restructure.

4) TRUE. The passage presents arguments both for and against the relaxation of pension rules about restructuring. Proponents believe that the current rule is: *obstructive to corporate activity.* The passage goes on to give the argument against relaxation as follows: *However, critics believe that this could give organisations carte blanche to shift their pension obligations to entities likely to become insolvent, thus forcing other organisations to subsidise their pension commitments.* These differing views confirm that the matter is indeed controversial.

5) CANNOT TELL. Although at the outset the passage clearly states that *many companies have acute shortfalls in their pension funds,* the question of whether or not the proposed legislation will help companies to reduce this shortfall is not discussed. Thus the answer to the question must be CANNOT TELL.

Practice test 8

TRUE	FALSE	CANNOT TELL
Answer **TRUE** if the statement is true or follows on logically from the passage.	Answer **FALSE** if the statement is false based ONLY on information in the passage.	Answer **CANNOT TELL** if there is insufficient information given in the passage.

Pill-Tech Pharmaceutical today announced its definitive agreement to purchase Sousa Labs, a privately owned biotechnology company, for $195 million. Hans Bitter, CEO of Pill-Tech, stated: 'Sousa Labs has the expertise – and now the resources – to develop new drugs for Pill-Tech based on genomics.' This is the third small biotech firm acquired by the pharmaceutical giant in as many months, an aggressive initiative fuelled by the impending patent expiration of four of Pill-Tech's best-selling drugs. One such medication, the antidepressant Dorvax, is responsible for a quarter of Pill-Tech's sales. Given the lengthy time frame and heavy expense of developing and marketing novel drugs, some industry analysts believe Pill-Tech should seek a merger partner with which to combine portfolios and cut operating costs. Despite questions over the company's ongoing acquisition strategy, its finances are solid with a market capitalisation of approximately $60 billion.

1) Pill-Tech's sales revenue will fall by a quarter as a consequence of the antidepressant Dorvax's patent expiry.
   TRUE/ FALSE/ CANNOT TELL

2) An alternative strategy for Pill-Tech's future would be to form an alliance with another large pharmaceutical company.
   TRUE/ FALSE/ CANNOT TELL

3) Uncertainty over Pill-Tech's future direction has had a negative impact on its economic position.
   TRUE/ FALSE/ CANNOT TELL

4)   Newly developed drugs will offset the lost sales when generic
      versions of their best-selling medicines become available.
      TRUE/ FALSE/ CANNOT TELL

5)   The passage suggests that it is likely that Pill-Tech will
      acquire more biotechnology companies.
      TRUE/ FALSE/ CANNOT TELL

Review your answers to practice test 8

1) CANNOT TELL. The passage says that *the antidepressant Dorvax is responsible for a quarter of Pill-Tech's sales.* However, Dorvax's patent expiry does not necessarily mean that sales revenue will fall by a quarter. There is no way of knowing for sure what will happen so the answer has to be CANNOT TELL.

2) TRUE. This is expressed in the passage as follows: *some industry analysts believe Pill-Tech should seek a merger partner with which to combine portfolios and cut operating costs.*

3) FALSE. The relevant part of the passage is: *Despite questions over the company's ongoing acquisition strategy,* **its finances are solid** *with a market capitalisation of approximately $60 billion.* This statement is not true because there has been no negative impact on Pill-Tech's economic position.

4) CANNOT TELL. This is tricky. The passage makes clear that Pill-Tech's strategy is to develop new drugs in order to compensate for lost sales as patents expire. However, the question says *will* and there is no way of knowing for certain whether or not this strategy will be effective, so the answer has to be CANNOT TELL.

5) TRUE. Look carefully at the last line of the passage: *Despite questions over the company's* **ongoing acquisition strategy***, its finances are solid with a market capitalisation of approximately $60 billion.* The word *ongoing* is key. It means that the company *is* likely to make more acquisitions in the future.

Practice test 9

TRUE	FALSE	CANNOT TELL
Answer **TRUE** if the statement is true or follows on logically from the passage.	Answer **FALSE** if the statement is false based ONLY on information in the passage.	Answer **CANNOT TELL** if there is insufficient information given in the passage.

An unprecedented escalation in oil prices is threatening the hegemony of long-distance global supply chains. The cost of shipping goods from overseas has risen by 40 per cent, thus eroding the competitive advantage of lower Asian wage costs. Companies that ship bulky, low-added-value goods are seeking alternative logistical solutions to reduce transport costs. One major manufacturer of paper products saved 500,000 gallons of fuel per year by relocating its distribution centres to facilitate shipping by rail. A switch to transporting wine by barge has enabled one supermarket chain to reduce its fleet of trucks by 5 per cent. Traditionally, American timber was shipped to China where it was made into furniture and then shipped back to the USA. But in the wake of rising energy costs, moribund domestic furniture-making centres are experiencing resurgence. Likewise, the American steel industry has seen production rise by 12 per cent while China's steel exports are down by a quarter.

1) Companies that ship light-weight, high-value products from overseas are immune to rising oil costs.
   TRUE/ FALSE/ CANNOT TELL

2) In certain industries a shift to domestic production is occurring.
   TRUE/ FALSE/ CANNOT TELL

3) America has always had a healthy furniture-making industry.
   TRUE/ FALSE/ CANNOT TELL

4)   American-produced steel is now cheaper than steel manu-
     factured in China.
     TRUE/ FALSE/ CANNOT TELL

5)   Given the current economic climate goods are no longer
     being produced in Asia for export overseas.
     TRUE/ FALSE/ CANNOT TELL

Review your answers to practice test 9

1) CANNOT TELL. The passage indicates that *Companies that ship bulky, low-added-value goods are seeking alternative logistical solutions to reduce transport costs.* But this does not mean that their opposite – light-weight, high-value items – are unaffected by rising oil costs.

2) TRUE. Two examples are given in the passage – the American furniture-making and steel industries.

3) FALSE. The passage describes the resurgence of *moribund* American furniture-making centres. So although they are now thriving, they were previously dormant, so it is incorrect to describe them as always healthy.

4) CANNOT TELL. The passage tells us that the American steel industry has benefited from rising oil prices with a 12 per cent rise in production. However, it is not possible – based on the information in the passage – to say whether or not American-produced steel is now cheaper than steel manufactured in China.

5) FALSE. The passage argues about the continuing economic viability for transporting goods long distance. Although some of the cost benefits have been eroded, this does not mean that it is no longer financially viable to manufacture goods in Asia. In fact, the passage states that *China's steel exports are down by a quarter.* So it logically follows that China is still exporting goods.

Practice test 10

TRUE	FALSE	CANNOT TELL
Answer **TRUE** if the statement is true or follows on logically from the passage.	Answer **FALSE** if the statement is false based ONLY on information in the passage.	Answer **CANNOT TELL** if there is insufficient information given in the passage.

An organisation's human capital is an intangible asset and as such is difficult to quantify. However, the average cost of voluntary defection can be conservatively estimated at £50,000 per employee, including the expense of recruitment and training. As a reduction in staff turnover equates to cost savings, HR practitioners in every industry are implementing retention programmes into their human capital management frameworks. Remuneration is no longer the simple solution to retaining valuable employees. In a recent survey of professionals, over 35 per cent of the respondents rated work/life balance as their primary career concern. One way for organisations to measure employee satisfaction is using attitudinal metrics, the data from which can be used to enact strategic change. The introduction of employee stock options is another way to increase a workforce's commitment and loyalty. When resources are limited, companies can design bespoke retention programmes for their highest-performing employees.

1) The passage suggests that financial compensation has been the primary way for organisations to retain high performers.
   TRUE/ FALSE/ CANNOT TELL

2) The cost of implementing a corporate retention scheme can be offset by saving on staff turnover.
   TRUE/ FALSE/ CANNOT TELL

3) Strategic change programmes are always based upon employee satisfaction survey results.
   TRUE/ FALSE/ CANNOT TELL

4) The passage suggests that company stock option schemes engender feelings of belonging amongst participants.
TRUE/ FALSE/ CANNOT TELL

Review your answers to practice test 10

1)   TRUE. The passage states that *Remuneration is **no longer** the simple solution to retaining valuable employees.* This implies that salary has traditionally been used to retain staff.

2)   CANNOT TELL. Do not be misled into thinking that this statement is true. The passage states: *As a reduction in staff turnover equates to cost savings, HR practitioners in every industry are implementing retention programmes into their human capital management frameworks.* However, this does not mean that one equals or offsets the other. More information is needed in order to compare the costs and savings.

3)   FALSE. The relevant part of the passage is as follows: ***One way** for organisations to measure employee satisfaction is using attitudinal metrics, the data from which can be used to enact strategic change.* This suggests that this is one of many ways to enact strategic change.

4)   TRUE. This is confirmed in the passage: *The introduction of employee stock options is another way to increase a workforce's commitment and loyalty.*

Practice test 11

TRUE	FALSE	CANNOT TELL
Answer **TRUE** if the statement is true or follows on logically from the passage.	Answer **FALSE** if the statement is false based ONLY on information in the passage.	Answer **CANNOT TELL** if there is insufficient information given in the passage.

Project management, the system of organising resources to achieve a finite long-term goal, contrasts starkly with process-based operations, such as traditional banking. When such process-based industries, which can be characterised by a functional execution of immediate tasks, embark on a project a clash of cultures almost inevitably ensues. But as the corporate world shifts towards an increasingly project-based model, managers within process-based businesses must be educated in project management. This does not simply mean training courses in the use of planning software, but rather the adoption of a completely different management methodology. Traditional hierarchies represent one challenge to project-based working, whereby the project's hierarchy supersedes organisational seniority. Another obstacle in reactive, process-based cultures is a resistance to planning, and a mindset that IT is peripheral, rather than integral, to business projects. These hurdles are indisputably worth overcoming, however, as acquiring project management capabilities enables businesses to function effectively in project mode while continuing to conduct their day-to-day operations efficiently.

1) When working on a project, senior staff might be accountable to a more junior project manager.
   TRUE/ FALSE/ CANNOT TELL

2) The passage indicates that project management methodologies are at odds with some industries.
   TRUE/ FALSE/ CANNOT TELL

3) Long-range planning is antithetical to the discipline of
   project management.
   TRUE/ FALSE/ CANNOT TELL

4) Training courses in planning software are sufficient for
   acquiring project management expertise.
   TRUE/ FALSE/ CANNOT TELL

5) The banking industry has resisted adopting project management methodologies.
   TRUE/ FALSE/ CANNOT TELL

Review your answers to practice test 11

1) TRUE. The following sentence is key: *Traditional hierarchies represent one challenge to project-based working,* **whereby the project's hierarchy supersedes organisational seniority**. Thus the project's leader could be overseeing the contributions of more senior staff members.

2) TRUE. The answer is true as the passage describes how project management *contrasts starkly with process-based operations, such as traditional banking.* The passage details the difficulties in overcoming cultural differences.

3) FALSE. The passage defines project management as *organising resources to achieve a finite long-term goal.* It is a system of long-range planning so the answer must be FALSE.

4) FALSE. The passage states: *This does* **not simply** *mean training courses in the use of planning software, but rather the adoption of a completely different management methodology.* Software training courses are certainly an important part of acquiring project management skills, but they are not sufficient – they need to be accompanied by a change in methodology.

5) CANNOT TELL. The passage cites banking as an example of a process-based industry. It also describes the difficulties involved in introducing such industries to project management techniques. However, no information specific to the banking industry is given, so it is impossible to say whether the industry has or has not resisted adopting project management methodologies.

Practice test 12

TRUE	FALSE	CANNOT TELL
Answer **TRUE** if the statement is true or follows on logically from the passage.	Answer **FALSE** if the statement is false based ONLY on information in the passage.	Answer **CANNOT TELL** if there is insufficient information given in the passage.

IT has been used commercially for over 50 years, yet no standard terminology or system for measuring the value of IT expenditure exists. This lack of methodology can be explained by IT's intangible nature and a prevailing belief that IT is a necessary, and uncontrollable, expense. Ultimately, any metric for assessing IT investment must determine whether it has increased income or decreased expenditure. It is far too simplistic to merely consider personnel cost savings resultant from IT investment. Similarly, to crudely define IT expenditure as only hardware, software and infrastructure would also be wrong – the time of managers and professionals must also be factored in. One of the main impediments to developing a process for analysing the cost/benefit of IT projects is a lack of ownership by senior management.

1) The passage outlines the predominant system for assessing the return on IT investment.
   TRUE/ FALSE/ CANNOT TELL

2) An obstacle to measuring IT investment is a lack of management responsibility for such projects.
   TRUE/ FALSE/ CANNOT TELL

3) The passage asserts that IT costs are intrinsically difficult to regulate.
   TRUE/ FALSE/ CANNOT TELL

4) One way of measuring an IT development success is whether it increases income for the business.
   TRUE/ FALSE/ CANNOT TELL

5)   The cost of IT professionals sometimes exceeds any per-
     sonnel costs savings resulting from an IT project.
     TRUE/ FALSE/ CANNOT TELL

Review your answers to practice test 12

1) FALSE. The opening sentence includes the phrase: *no standard terminology or system for measuring the value of IT expenditure exists.* The passage describes the difficulties in assessing IT investment, rather than outlining a system.

2) TRUE. The passage states that *One of the main impediments to developing a process for analysing the cost/benefit of IT projects is **a lack of ownership by senior management**.*

3) TRUE. The passage states that: *This lack of methodology can be explained by IT's intangible nature and a prevailing belief that IT is a necessary, and uncontrollable, expense.* These two factors make IT costs difficult to regulate.

4) TRUE. The passage says: *Ultimately, any metric for assessing IT investment must determine whether it has **increased income** or decreased expenditure.* Two ways of measuring IT investment are given, and one of these is increased income.

5) CANNOT TELL. The passage states that IT investment can result in personnel savings. In the second-to-last sentence it also reminds us that IT staff costs must be factored in. So both the cost of IT professionals and savings on personnel are factors to be considered when measuring success. However, no direct cost comparison is given, so it is not possible to ascertain whether one exceeds the other (even though it is likely that this probably *is* the case sometimes).

Practice test 13

TRUE	FALSE	CANNOT TELL
Answer **TRUE** if the statement is true or follows on logically from the passage.	Answer **FALSE** if the statement is false based ONLY on information in the passage.	Answer **CANNOT TELL** if there is insufficient information given in the passage.

The Far Eastern practical philosophy of Confucianism did not begin as a religion and, unlike other religious institutions, does not have a clergy or church associated with it. It has been followed for two millennia in China and was the state orthodoxy until the Chinese Revolution in 1911. Whilst it is not an organised religion, Confucianism is still hugely influential on East Asian spiritual and political life. Confucius taught a way of living one's life through adopting moral values as the basis for political and social actions, firmly focusing on one's family foundations within the community. There are two ethical divisions in Confucianism: the first derives from Confucius himself, and values following conventional codes of behaviour; the second strand came from medieval neo-Confucians' belief in following one's moral intuitions.

1) Confucius created an ethical division in Confucianism.
   TRUE/ FALSE/ CANNOT TELL

2) Confucianism has been practised in China for hundreds of years.
   TRUE/ FALSE/ CANNOT TELL

3) Confucianism is a religion that values the family over the community.
   TRUE/ FALSE/ CANNOT TELL

4) Confucianism is both a religion and a system of philosophy.
   TRUE/ FALSE/ CANNOT TELL

5) Confucianism is not practised outside of the Far East.
   TRUE/ FALSE/ CANNOT TELL

Review your answers to practice test 13

1) FALSE. The last sentence in the passage states that there
   are two ethical divisions in Confucianism. The first is the
   original form, coming from Confucius himself. The division
   came about at a later date, and Confucius was not responsible for it. This passage says: *the second strand came from
   medieval neo-Confucians' belief in following one's moral intuitions.* Confucius lived *circa* 550 BC; the medieval period
   was over a thousand years later. However, you don't need to
   know these dates in order to answer the question correctly –
   the sentence clearly states that the division wasn't his doing.

2) TRUE. In explaining the origins of Confucianism, the
   passage states that *It has been followed for two millennia in
   China.*

3) CANNOT TELL. The passage suggests that Confucianism
   values both family and community, and it is not possible to
   say whether one has greater importance than the other.
   *Confucius taught a way of living one's life through adopting
   moral values as the basis for political and social actions, firmly
   focusing on one's family foundations within the community.*

4) TRUE. The passage tells us that Confucianism started out
   as a philosophy: *The Far Eastern **practical philosophy** of
   Confucianism did not begin as a religion and, **unlike other
   religious institutions**, does not have a clergy or church
   associated with it.* However, the phrase '*unlike other religious
   institutions*' suggests that Confucianism is also a religion,
   albeit one without a formal church connected to it.

5) CANNOT TELL. The passage states: *Confucianism is still
   hugely influential on East Asian spiritual and political life.* So
   you may be tempted to answer TRUE. Equally, you may
   know people who don't live in the Far East yet practise

Confucianism and be tempted to answer FALSE. In fact, the correct answer is CANNOT TELL, because information on where Confucianism is practised is not given in the passage.

Practice test 14

TRUE	FALSE	CANNOT TELL
Answer **TRUE** if the statement is true or follows on logically from the passage.	Answer **FALSE** if the statement is false based ONLY on information in the passage.	Answer **CANNOT TELL** if there is insufficient information given in the passage.

The ancients had many ingenious methods for measuring time. Water clocks, for example, were used in ancient Greek and Rome to time orators' speeches. One version comprised pouring water into a hollow cylinder or glass jar. As water flowed through, measuring lines established the extent of time that had passed. Sundials are another early form of clock. They consist of a central stylus that uses the Sun's rays to cast a shadow on to a horizontal dial plate and hence to show the local Sun time. As with water clocks, sundials needed to be calibrated in order to show the passage of time. Prior to the development of sundials, stones or poles could be placed in the ground. In addition to their water clocks and sundials, the ancient Egyptians used obelisks and pyramids to tell the time from the passage of the sun.

1)   The ancient Egyptians calibrated sundials in a similar fashion to water clocks.
     TRUE/ FALSE/ CANNOT TELL

2)   Upright stones were one forerunner of sundials.
     TRUE/ FALSE/ CANNOT TELL

3)   The primary use for water clocks was to time speeches.
     TRUE/ FALSE/ CANNOT TELL

4)   Water clocks were only used in ancient Greece and Rome.
     TRUE/ FALSE/ CANNOT TELL

5)   The passage states that the ancient Egyptians built obelisks for telling the time.
     TRUE/ FALSE/ CANNOT TELL

Review your answers to practice test 14

1) CANNOT TELL. Although the passage clearly states that both sundials and water clocks needed to be calibrated, it does not specify *how* each was calibrated – so it is impossible to determine whether both were calibrated in the same way.

2) TRUE. The second-to-last sentence reveals that prior to the development of sundials, stones or poles were placed in the ground to mark the time.

3) CANNOT TELL. The second sentence states that *Water clocks, for example, were used in ancient Greek and Rome to time orators' speeches.* So while it is true that this is how water clocks were sometimes used, it is not possible to determine whether it was their *primary* purpose.

4) FALSE. The last sentence mentions that water clocks were used in ancient Egypt, and it is possible that they were used in other places too.

5) FALSE. The last sentence says that *the ancient Egyptians used obelisks and pyramids to tell the time from the passage of the sun.* While obelisks could be used for time-telling, it does not necessarily follow that that was the reason they were built – and nowhere does the passage suggest this.

Practice test 15

TRUE	FALSE	CANNOT TELL
Answer **TRUE** if the statement is true or follows on logically from the passage.	Answer **FALSE** if the statement is false based ONLY on information in the passage.	Answer **CANNOT TELL** if there is insufficient information given in the passage.

Whereas invertebrates have an external exoskeleton, humans and other vertebrates have an internal endoskeleton. The human endoskeleton is comprised of cartilage and the body's 206 bones, which are connected to each other by ligaments. As well as protecting and supporting the body's internal organs, the human endoskeleton also works in conjunction with muscles, joints and the nervous system to enable movement. Joints occur between bones, making the skeleton flexible by acting as hinges or pivots. Tendons attach muscles to bones and contract in response to a stimulus from the body's nervous system. Those muscles that are under conscious control, the skeletal muscles, act by pulling against the bones of the skeleton.

1) Physical activity requires the muscles and bones to synchronise.
   TRUE/ FALSE/ CANNOT TELL

2) The human endoskeleton provides connection points for the body's muscles.
   TRUE/ FALSE/ CANNOT TELL

3) The human skeleton is comprised mainly of bone.
   TRUE/ FALSE/ CANNOT TELL

4) Unlike invertebrates, humans have an internal exoskeleton.
   TRUE/ FALSE/ CANNOT TELL

5) Bones contract skeletal muscles in response to signals from the nervous system.
   TRUE/ FALSE/ CANNOT TELL

Review your answers to practice test 15

1) TRUE. The third sentence in the paragraph states that *the human endoskeleton also works in conjunction with muscles, joints and the nervous system to enable movement*. So bones (i.e. the endoskeleton) must work together (i.e. synchronise) with muscles for physical activity to occur.

2) TRUE. In the fifth sentence the reader is told that *Tendons attach muscles to bones*.

3) CANNOT TELL. The second sentence states that *The human endoskeleton is comprised of cartilage and the body's 206 bones*. Common sense might lead you to answer true, but remember, you must answer based only on what is in the passage – and it does not specify which percentage is bone as compared to cartilage.

4) FALSE. This is not a difficult question, but it is easy to get it wrong if you read it too quickly. Humans have an internal *endoskeleton*, not exoskeleton, as specified in the first sentence.

5) FALSE. As explained in the passage's final two sentences, it is the body's muscles that contract in response to nerve stimuli and pull against the bones.

Practice test 16

TRUE	FALSE	CANNOT TELL
Answer **TRUE** if the statement is true or follows on logically from the passage.	Answer **FALSE** if the statement is false based ONLY on information in the passage.	Answer **CANNOT TELL** if there is insufficient information given in the passage.

The Copernican model of the solar system, with the Earth and associated planets revolving around the Sun, was formulated in the middle of the sixteenth century. Nicolaus Copernicus's theory was the first heliocentric model of planetary motion, placing the sun at the centre. That said, his solar model retained the erroneous premise – as per the Ptolemaic System – that planets move in perfect circles. The sixteenth century's move away from the geocentric view of the universe as being centred on Earth led to a complete change in people's concept of the universe. The Copernican model of the solar system laid the groundwork for Newton's laws of gravity and Kepler's laws of planetary motion. The former describes how planets are held in their individual orbits.

1) The passage suggests that the Copernican system was flawless.
    TRUE/ FALSE/ CANNOT TELL

2) Copernicus developed the first geocentric model of the Earth's solar system.
    TRUE/ FALSE/ CANNOT TELL

3) Copernicus paved the way for Newton's work on the orbits of the planets.
    TRUE/ FALSE/ CANNOT TELL

4) The Ptolemaic system preceded the Copernican model.
    TRUE/ FALSE/ CANNOT TELL

5) Nicolaus Copernicus's work in the 1600s had a profound effect on how the universe was understood.
    TRUE/ FALSE/ CANNOT TELL

Review your answers to practice test 16

1) FALSE. The passage states that mistakes remained in the Copernican system: *That said, his solar model retained the erroneous premise – as per the Ptolemaic System – that planets move in perfect circles.*

2) FALSE. The second sentence states: *Nicolaus Copernicus's theory was the first heliocentric model of planetary motion, placing the sun at the centre.* Thus, his model was heliocentric rather than geocentric.

3) TRUE. This statement paraphrases the last two sentences. The penultimate sentence says that Copernicus's work influenced Newton, while the final sentence states that Newton's work explained how planets stay in their orbit.

4) TRUE. In the third sentence the passage says: *That said, his solar model retained the erroneous premise – as per the Ptolemaic System – that planets move in perfect circles.* The word *retained* lets us know that the Ptolemaic System came before the Copernican model.

5) FALSE. While it is true that Nicolaus Copernicus's planetary model profoundly changed how the universe was perceived, as stated in the fourth sentence, he did not work in the 1600s, but in the sixteenth century (i.e. the 1500s).

Practice test 17

TRUE	FALSE	CANNOT TELL
Answer **TRUE** if the statement is true or follows on logically from the passage.	Answer **FALSE** if the statement is false based ONLY on information in the passage.	Answer **CANNOT TELL** if there is insufficient information given in the passage.

For something that is everywhere, colour is often misunderstood. The sensation of colour is a consequence of the human eye reacting differently to different wavelengths of light. Thus colour is not actually the property of an object. Any colour can be created by combining the three primary colours. An object that absorbs all light wavelengths appears black, whilst one that reflects all wavelengths is white. Some colours have different associations depending on where you are in the world. Purple, for example, is associated with royalty in Western societies. In Thailand, however, it is the colour of mourning. The meanings of colours can also change over time. Today, in Western culture, baby girls are often dressed in pink. In the 19th century, however, pink was seen as a colour for baby boys.

1) Black objects reflect all light wavelengths.
   TRUE/ FALSE/ CANNOT TELL

2) The colour red is perceived differently in Western society to how it is viewed in Asian cultures.
   TRUE/ FALSE/ CANNOT TELL

3) Colour is a ubiquitous sensation.
   TRUE/ FALSE/ CANNOT TELL

4) In Western culture, pink has traditionally been viewed as a feminine hue.
   TRUE/ FALSE/ CANNOT TELL

5) The passage argues that colour is often misunderstood because everyone's eyes perceive light differently.
   TRUE/ FALSE/ CANNOT TELL

Review your answers to practice test 17

1) FALSE. The opposite is stated in the passage: *An object that absorbs all light wavelengths appears black, whilst one that reflects all wavelengths is white.*

2) CANNOT TELL. This is quite likely, as evidenced by the sentence: *Some colours have different associations depending on where you are in the world.* An example is provided of the colour purple; however, no example is given for the colour red – so there is no way of knowing for sure whether red is viewed differently in Asia to the way it is viewed in Western culture.

3) TRUE. Colour is everywhere – i.e. ubiquitous – and is also described in the passage as follows: *The **sensation** of colour is a consequence of the human eye reacting differently to different wavelengths of light.*

4) FALSE. The last two sentences provide an example of how the cultural associations of colour can change over time. *Today, in Western culture, baby girls are often dressed in pink. In the 19th century, however, pink was seen as a colour for baby boys.* Although it is now seen as a feminine colour in Western society, it has not always been so.

5) FALSE. While the passage states that colour is often mis-understood in the first sentence, it does not attribute this to individual differences in perceiving light.

CHAPTER 9

Critical reasoning tests

As in the previous two chapters, the critical reasoning tests in this chapter feature a passage-based format. However, in a critical reasoning test the passages are longer, and much more complex in terms of subject matter and language. Furthermore, the questions related to the passage take a variety of formats and require you to make deductions and inferences, and to summarise points being made in the passage.

Critical reasoning tests are the most advanced form of verbal reasoning test and are typically taken by candidates for senior managerial roles. Passages are usually set in a financial or business context appropriate to the role being applied for. The practice tests in this chapter are also at an equivalent level of difficulty to the LNAT's verbal critical reasoning test, which is taken by applicants to British law schools.

In recent years, the situational judgement test (SJT) has become increasingly commonplace. One of the attractions is that rather than measuring verbal reasoning it is possible to create SJT scenarios which measure many different skills – particularly those involved in effective judgement/decision-making, team working and prioritisation. This book is not intended to cover SJTs. There are some useful practice SJTs, by competency – as found in real situational judgement tests – at this URL: www.assessment.com/test

Instructions

Read the passage of text and then answer the set of questions associated with the passage. Once you've completed the practice test, check your answers against the answer explanations that follow the test. Be sure to cover the answers up while you are taking the test!

> **brilliant tip**
>
> Skim read the passage initially to get a feel for the main points. Then re-read the passage more carefully, mentally noting the key content of each paragraph.

Critical reasoning practice test 1 – passage

The extreme cold and wet weather events of late 2013/early 2014 in the US and the UK respectively brought the clear links to climate change back into the political arena. Prior to this the UK government's focus was on other political and socio-economic issues such as unemployment and a very welcome – however uneven – recovery. Yet, in the same period of the credit crunch and its aftermath, the US's home-grown 'fracking' industry revolutionised America's energy economy. American 'fracking' now looks to deliver a supply of cheap gas for many years to come. Over the same period, the world's second biggest economic powerhouse, China, has further cemented its reputation for exporting solar power technologies. By 2015, the US expects to be energy self-sufficient and to have become the world's biggest oil producer.

Britain's Energy Minister has described fracking as 'an exciting prospect, which could bring faster growth, more jobs and energy security'. Already drilling rights covering almost 40,000 British square miles have been sold to 'fracking' companies who will from 2014 apply for the additional environmental and planning permits that are required before any drilling can proceed. The British government only expects a minority of these exploration rights to be claimed. Fracking has already started in West Sussex, causing a massive increase in road traffic and in opponents campaigning on site against the potential environmental damage. In fact, fracking is banned in France for environmental reasons.

Fracking in the US involves pumping sand, water and special chemicals into the ground to widen the cracks where pockets of gas are trapped. This solution then needs to be pumped out before collecting the released gas. The UK hopes that US-style fracking methods will produce a US-style 'revolt' in the price of domestic energy. The American desire for cheaper energy is driving an *onshoring* process that is shifting manufacturing bases back home from the Far East. This reindustrialisation has helped to underpin a rapidly improving US recovery.

Practice test 1 - questions

1) Which of the following is the most accurate summary of the second paragraph?
   a) Drilling rights across the UK are expected to lead to a rapid expansion of fracking.
   b) Environmental activists recently lost their fight to stop fracking coming to the UK.
   c) The British government is broadly supportive of more fracking across the UK.
   d) There are economic and environmental benefits from increasing our use of fracking.
   e) Fracking has recently begun in the UK and there is economic support for its future expansion.

2) Which of the following statements can be inferred from the passage?
   a) America is one of the world's key manufacturers of solar power equipment.
   b) The British fracking industry is nascent.
   c) Fracking is an increasingly contentious means of extracting gas across the globe.
   d) Social unrest is caused by high levels of unemployment.
   e) The latest global recession is now over.

3) What does the passage's author intend to show by putting the word 'revolt' in inverted commas?
   a) That he disagrees.
   b) To show that this is a quote.
   c) The revolt was unplanned.
   d) The revolt may not have happened.
   e) It was an unusual revolt.

4)   The passage includes which one or more of the following facts about fracking in the US?

a) There has been rapidly rising US unemployment due to the global recession.

b) The first British fracking sites were established in West Sussex in 2013.

c) The US imports most of its manufactured goods from the Far East.

d) Fracking has caused a shift in US energy prices.

e) Exploration rights have been sold for over 40,000 square miles of land.

5)   What is the meaning of the *onshoring* term used in the context of the final paragraph?

a) The trade deficit between America and the Far East has reduced.

b) Many Americans prefer to use cheaper, onshored energy.

c) The pumping of a mixture of sand, water and special chemicals into the ground.

d) Bringing goods manufacturing back to America.

e) The rapid improvement in American industry.

6)   Which of the following best summarises the passage's main idea?

a) Fracking's benefits clearly outweigh the costs.

b) The UK is aiming to mirror the US's fracking expansion.

c) The price of gas fluctuates over time.

d) Fracking could potentially alter the UK's energy supply mix.

e) The politically charged economic benefits of fracking have environmental costs.

Review your answers to practice test 1

1) *Which of the following is the most accurate summary of the second paragraph?* This is an example of an interpretation type of verbal critical reasoning question. It is asking you to précis the second paragraph into a single sentence which is a more concise – but still representative – summary of the paragraph. The second paragraph starts with an upbeat quote from Britain's Energy Minister, then describes the drilling rights sales process: both what has happened so far and what is expected in the near future. The last two sentences detail some of the downsides to the issue of fracking expansion which has led to a French ban for environmental reasons. It's an effective strategy for this type of critical thinking question to consider each of the answer options on its own merits. Whilst this might seem to be an inefficient approach, the question does ask you to find *the most* accurate summary.

a) *Drilling rights across the UK are expected to lead to a rapid expansion of fracking.* This statement is false. The passage states that *The British government only expects a minority of these exploration rights to be claimed.*

b) *Environmental activists recently lost their fight to stop fracking coming to the UK.* This is a statement of fact. However, it only covers one of the key points made by the passage and so cannot be the *most accurate summary*.

c) *The British government is broadly supportive of more fracking across the UK.* This statement summarises a couple of the key points from the passage, although since it omits other key points it is not broadly representative. It is therefore unlikely to be *the most accurate summary*.

d) *There are economic and environmental benefits from increasing our use of fracking.* This statement is false; no environmental benefits are mentioned in the passage – quite the opposite in fact.

e) ***Fracking has recently begun in the UK and there is economic support for its future expansion.*** This is the best answer since it is a more accurate summary than (b).

2) *Which of the following statements can be inferred from the passage?* This is an example of an inference type of critical thinking question. Such an inference is derived from logical conclusions. It is based on facts presented in the passage, even though the inferred statement itself will *not* appear in the passage. OK, let's go through each of the answer options one at a time as we did with the first question to see which is an inference from the passage.

a) *America is one of the world's key manufacturers of solar power equipment.* The only mention of solar power in the passage is: *China has further cemented its reputation for exporting solar power technologies.* It is China and not America that is *one of the world's key manufacturers of solar power equipment.* So answer option (a) is incorrect.

b) ***The British fracking industry is nascent.*** The word 'nascent' means being born and then starting to grow. It's clear from the passage that the British fracking industry has recently started and will expand to an as yet unknown extent. Hence this statement can be inferred from the passage, which makes answer option (b) the correct answer.

c) *Fracking is an increasingly contentious means of extracting gas across the globe.* This statement is inferring that there is an increasing amount of resistance to fracking. Whilst there is resistance in Britain it cannot be inferred that globally it is becoming *increasingly contentious.*

d) *Social unrest is caused by high levels of unemployment.* This is a cause and effect statement which cannot be inferred from the passage.

e) *The latest global recession is now over.* No mention is made of the global recession finishing, hence answer option (e) is incorrect.

3) *What does the passage's author intend to show by putting the word 'revolt' in inverted commas?* This is an example of an interpretation type of critical thinking question. The most efficient means of answering this question is to quickly review the answer options and eliminate those such as (b) *To show that this is a quote* and (d) *The revolt may not have happened,* which are clearly not the case. Of the remaining answer options (a) *That he disagrees* just doesn't make sense in the context of the passage. Also, (c) *The revolt was unplanned* seems irrelevant, hence unlikely to be the author's point.

Answer option (d) is unlikely. So does answer option (e) **It was an unusual revolt** make sense in that part of the passage where the term 'revolt' is used? Earlier in the passage a US revolution due to fracking is mentioned, then later the passage considers the hopes of the UK for a *US-style 'revolt' in the price of domestic energy.* Both uses are a weaker form of the words *revolution* and *revolt,* which typically refer to a significant socio-political shift. In this sense the revolt was indeed an *unusual* one. Thus answer option (e) is correct.

4) *The passage includes which one or more of the following facts about fracking in the US?* This is a more traditional type of question found in many different types of verbal reasoning test. Similar to the True/False/Cannot tell question format described in earlier chapters; here you need to find which one of the five statements is True. It's worth reviewing each option quickly and if you can't recall specific mention of this potential fact in the passage, then that's all that you need to know (since it can't therefore be true).

a) *There has been rapidly rising US unemployment due to the global recession.* There is no specific information in the passage. This part of the passage has a different emphasis: *American desire for cheaper energy is driving an onshoring process that is shifting manufacturing bases back home from the Far East.*

b) *The first British fracking sites were established in West Sussex in 2013.* This is tricky and highlights the importance of reading each question very carefully, as well as rereading the relevant part of the passage. Certainly *fracking has already started in West Sussex.* It is easy to assume from this statement's context – the onset of fracking in the UK – that the first British fracking sites must be in West Sussex. This is not necessarily true though.

c) *The US imports most of its manufactured goods from the Far East.* This part of the passage has a different emphasis: *American desire for cheaper energy is driving an onshoring process that is shifting manufacturing bases back home from the Far East.* Based on all the passage's information, the statement is not true.

d) **Fracking has caused a shift in US energy prices.** American fracking now looks to deliver a supply of cheap gas, thus answer option (d) is correct.

e) *Exploration rights have been sold for over 40,000 square miles of land.* The relevant part of the passage refers to *almost* 40,000 British square miles – not *over* 40,000 square miles of land. The statement is false.

5) *What is the meaning of the onshoring term used in the context of the final paragraph?* This is an example of a comprehension type of verbal critical reasoning question. It is asking you what the term means and hints that the context of the final paragraph will help you (if you don't already know the word's meaning). Here are the last two sentences in the passage: *The American desire for cheaper energy is*

driving an onshoring process that is shifting manufacturing bases back home from the Far East. This reindustrialisation has helped to underpin a rapidly improving US recovery. Of the available answer options, which meaning for the term *onshoring* best fits within the context of these final sentences?

a) *The trade deficit between America and the Far East has reduced.* Possibly.

b) *Many Americans prefer to use cheaper, onshored energy.* This is not mentioned specifically in the passage.

c) *The pumping of a mixture of sand, water and special chemicals into the ground.* Not mentioned in these two sentences.

d) **Bringing goods manufacturing back to America.** This meaning works since the passage mentions *shifting manufacturing bases back home from the Far East.* Hence answer option (d) is the correct answer.

e) *The rapid improvement in American industry.* This is not mentioned specifically in the passage.

6) *Which of the following best summarises the passage's main idea?* The statements (a), (c) and (d) are not summaries of the passage. Although statement (b) is a summary of parts of the passage, it is not as effective a summary as (e) **The politically charged economic benefits of fracking have environmental costs.**

Critical reasoning practice test 2 - passage

Although the human genome was mapped many years ago, only now are we starting to see the expected medical advances. Watson and Crick's original understanding of DNA was, first, that our genes control all of our physical characteristics and susceptibility to disease; and secondly, that genes do not change over time. Whilst this without doubt was one of biology's most influential discoveries many modern geneticists now question the intransigence of human genes.

Evidence is increasing for the human mind–body connection being extended right down to the genetic level. 'Epigenetics' is the scientific name assigned to this rapidly expanding field. More specifically, *epigenetics* is how this activity changes in response to our life experiences. Genetics and evolutionary theory have traditionally treated genetic mutation as entirely random. However, this new paradigm of 'self-directed biological transformation' rewrites our long-standing rules for genetic mutation. In today's new world of *epigenetics*, '*self-directed biological transformation*' models how the human genome adapts in response to its environment.

The human genome can respond to everything that we experience. The human genome's environment is all our thoughts, feelings, and every other stimulus picked up by our five senses. So even if you engage in traditionally healthy activities such as yoga and meditation, these will immediately stimulate a response in genetic activity. There are major shifts in cellular activity leading to physiological changes. Exercise, a balanced diet, good sleep, and stress reduction – all well-known for improving bodily function – exert beneficial effects via our genes. This is another research finding that surprised many geneticists. It's also another challenge to the traditional 'biology as destiny' perspective in which our destiny was genetically defined from birth.

The next frontier will be to discover how deep and lasting such changes are, how much control we have over them individually, and how they can be passed on to future generations through so-called soft inheritance, in which the parents' life experiences and behaviour directly influence the genome of their offspring – transmitted via the epigenome, which controls how the activities of our genes are turned up and down.

Practice test 2 – questions

1) What does the passage's author mean when describing inheritance as 'soft'?
   a) gentle
   b) parental
   c) not genetic
   d) expedient
   e) transgenerational

2) Which of the following words are the best substitute for 'paradigm of' in the second paragraph?
   a) structure for
   b) dimension to
   c) model of
   d) test for
   e) human anatomy, theory of

3) Which of the following is *not* described as beneficial?
   a) jogging
   b) meditation
   c) diet
   d) yoga
   e) exercise

4) Which of the following is not discussed in the passage?
   a) Environmental effects on the human genome.
   b) What is and isn't genetically defined from birth.
   c) The epigenome's activity.
   d) Modern theories of genetics.
   e) Watson and Crick's early genetics research.

Review your answers to practice test 2

1) *What does the passage's author mean when describing inheritance as 'soft'?* The context of the passage reveals that 'soft' is being used to highlight that this is not 'hard' inheritance. In other words (c) **Not genetic**.

2) *Which of the following words are the best substitute for 'paradigm of' in the second paragraph?* The best substitute is answer option (c) **Model of**.

3) *Which of the following is not described as beneficial?* On reading the question, the relevant sentence that comes to mind is: *Exercise, a balanced diet, good sleep, and stress reduction – all well-known for improving bodily function – exert beneficial effects via our genes.* However, a more cautious approach is warranted since there is a second relevant sentence: . . . *engage in traditionally healthy activities such as yoga and meditation.* Once you have retraced this information in the passage, it's obvious that the only option that's not listed is (a) ***Jogging***.

4) *Which of the following is not discussed in the passage?* Going through each answer option, the following are mentioned in the passage: (a) Environmental effects on the human genome; (c) The epigenome's activity; (d) Modern theories of genetics; and (e) Watson and Crick's early genetics research. Thus the remaining answer option is logically the only possible correct one: (b) **What is and isn't genetically defined from birth**. Genetic and non-genetic factors are not detailed in the passage.

Critical reasoning practice test 3 – passage

The human activity in which we spend the highest proportion of our time is sleeping. Like humans, every other animal species relies upon regular sleep; to the extent that sleep deprivation can result in death. This makes it all the more surprising that there is no unifying theory to explain why we need to sleep, or why we dream. There is actually much controversy amongst sleep researchers: on the one side are those favouring a memory-based unifying theory to explain sleep, whereas, on the other side of the debate are those sleep researchers who believe that toxins are cleared from the brain during sleep. In fact, neuroscientific research now focuses on these two related questions: (i) What is the human brain doing whilst we sleep; and (ii) Why did human sleep evolve? This second question is particularly puzzling, given that whenever an animal sleeps it is at the mercy of any other animal predators out hunting. It would be an enormous advantage for any animal to not have to sleep. Regardless of the hazards whilst asleep, every single type of animal species does sleep. So sleep must therefore bestow something vital.

Over the last 3.5 billion years on Earth, animal species have evolved their individual biological clocks in response to the alternating cycles of natural light from the sun. It makes some evolutionary sense for human brains to use the regular down-time period of sleep to refresh themselves by clearing out toxins and restoring energy levels. During the day the brain streams in data from all our senses and this huge amount of data needs to be processed at night. So sleep *probably* serves all these functions.

Question (i) addresses the physiology of the brain during sleep. There are four stages of non-REM sleep in a typical sleeping cycle, with these regular cycles repeated up to five times a night. Dreaming only occurs during the fifth stage, which is character-ised by 'rapid eye movements', or REM sleep.

Most adults and children, if woken during REM sleep, will report that they were dreaming. It's during this dreaming REM phase that your body is paralysed – except for the eye muscles. During REM sleep is the only time that the stress-related chemical, noradrenalin, is switched off in the brain. This allows the brain to remain calm as particularly emotional events from the day before are reprocessed. Each night, during our few hours of deep sleep, our brain moves our memories from short-term to long-term storage, thus freeing-up short-term memory space for tomorrow. Our memories do need to be consolidated within 24 hours of being formed, so without sufficient deep sleep, some unconsolidated memories are eventually lost.

Most REM sleep occurs in the last half of the night. Hence, the effect of feeling stressed and groggy if you're woken up in the middle of REM sleep by a sudden noise. Your brain has not yet processed all of your difficult emotions from the previous day.

Francis Crick – who with Watson discovered the double helix structure of DNA – posited that non-REM sleep was to replenish the body, whilst REM sleep was to replenish the brain. A more recent theory to explain dreaming posits that a 'sleeping' brain is actually piecing together an information jigsaw of that day's events to get clarity of the picture as a whole. This theory conveniently explains the bizarre associations that occur in dreams as due to anomalous pieces of information that do not readily 'fit'.

If you cut back on sleep then this first causes those genes associated with your immune and stress responses to became more active. Secondly, there is increased activity in your genes which are associated with diabetes and cancer. However, additional sleep decreases activity in all these genes.

Practice test 3 - questions

1) All of the following aspects of sleep are discussed by the author in the first paragraph except for which one?
   a) human sleep
   b) sleeping hazard
   c) REM sleep
   d) sleep evolution
   e) predators sleeping

2) Which of the following statements can be inferred from the passage?
   a) There are unanswered questions about the reasons for sleep.
   b) DNA has a double-helix structure.
   c) REM sleep is one of the most important sleep stages.
   d) Both body and mind may be replenished during different sleep stages.

3) Which of the following is *not* characteristic of REM sleep?
   a) memory transfer
   b) events reprocessing
   c) complete paralysis
   d) lack of noradrenalin
   e) dreams

4) Which of the following possible explanations for sleep's evolution are not present in the passage?
   a) It replenishes energy levels.
   b) It replenishes the body and the brain.
   c) It allows sense to be made of the day's events.
   d) It clears the brain of toxins.
   e) It keeps animals safe from predators.

5) The passage includes which one or more of the following facts about sleep?

a) Not sleeping for a few days can slowly cause someone to die from exhaustion.

b) Neuroscience has failed to answer the most basic questions about sleep.

c) Non-REM and REM sleep tend to alternate.

d) The Earth has been inhabited by animals for 3.5 billion years.

e) A typical human spends most of the 24-hour day to night cycle engaged in dreams.

Review your answers to practice test 3

1) *All of the following aspects of sleep are discussed by the author in the first paragraph except for which one?* There must be four answer options which are included in the first paragraph, leaving one answer option that is not mentioned. These four are highlighted in bold below:

   *Why did **human sleep evolve**? This second question is particularly puzzling, given that whenever an animal sleeps it is at the mercy of any **other animal predators out hunting**. It would be an enormous advantage for any animal to not have to sleep. Regardless of the **hazards whilst asleep**, every single type of animal species does sleep. So sleep must therefore bestow something vital.*

   The unmentioned and therefore correct answer is answer option (c) **REM sleep.**

2) *Which of these statements can be inferred from the passage?* This is an example of an inference type of critical thinking question. Taking each of the answer options one at a time:

   a) *There are unanswered questions about sleep.* There are several places in the passage from which it can be inferred that there is an unanswered question about sleep, including: *neuroscientific research now focuses on these two related questions. . . This second question is particularly puzzling. . . So sleep probably serves all these functions.*

   b) *DNA has a double-helix structure.* This is true according to the passage: *Francis Crick – who with Watson discovered the double helix structure.*

   c) *REM sleep is one of the most important sleep stages.* The passage mentions several facts highlighting the importance of REM sleep, including that this is when dreaming occurs. Hence this statement can be inferred from the passage.

   d) *Both body and mind may be replenished during different sleep stages.* This statement is referring to Crick's theory (in the next-to-last paragraph): *non-REM sleep was to replenish the body, whilst REM sleep was to replenish the brain.* It can therefore be inferred from the passage.

3) *Which of the following is* not *characteristic of REM sleep?* Four of the answer options are described in the passage. By a process of elimination, the only one that isn't is (c) **Complete paralysis**. *It's during this dreaming REM phase that your body is paralysed – except for the eye muscles.*

4) *Which of the following possible explanations for sleep's evolution are not present in the passage?* Taking the answer options one at a time to exclude each of those that are found in the passage:

   a) *It replenishes energy levels.* This explanation is given in the passage: *use the regular downtime period of sleep to restore energy levels.*

   b) *Both body and mind may be replenished during different sleep stages.* This is given as a possible explanation in the passage: *refresh themselves by clearing out toxins.*

   c) *It allows sense to be made of the day's events.* This explanation is given in two places within the passage: *this huge amount of data needs to be processed at night . . .* and later, *piecing together an information jigsaw of that day's events to get clarity of the picture as a whole.*

   d) *It clears the brain of toxins.* This is given as a possible explanation in the passage: *refresh themselves by clearing out toxins.*

   e) *It keeps animals safe from predators.* This is not mentioned specifically in the passage. In fact, the opposite can be inferred from the passage. Hence (e) is the correct answer.

5)   *The passage includes which one or more of the following facts about REM sleep?* This is a comprehension type of verbal critical reasoning question. So, taking the answer options one at a time:

a) **Not sleeping for a few days can slowly cause someone to die from exhaustion.** This fact is described in: *sleep deprivation can result in death.*

b) *Neuroscience has failed to answer the most basic questions about sleep.* The following describes this: *neuroscientific research now focuses on these two related questions.* However, answer option (b) is still not a fact.

c) **Non-REM and REM sleep tend to alternate.** This fact is found in the following part of the passage: *four stages of non-REM sleep in a typical sleeping cycle, with these regular cycles repeated up to five times a night.*

d) **The Earth has been inhabited by animals for 3.5 billion years.** The following describes this fact: *Over the last 3.5 billion years on Earth, animal species have evolved . . .*

e) **A typical human spends most of the 24-hour day–night cycle engaged in dreams.** This fact is found in the first sentence of the passage: *The human activity in which we spend the highest proportion of our time is sleeping.*

What did you think of this book?

We're really keen to hear from you about this book, so that we can make our publishing even better.

Please log on to the following website and leave us your feedback.

It will only take a few minutes and your thoughts are invaluable to us.

www.pearsoned.co.uk/bookfeedback